SO-BZW-180

Sadlier
CHRIST IN US™

Parish Edition 1

"*Christ In Us* Grade 1 cover artwork speaks
to the children's discovery of their loving
relationships within their families."

Reverend Donald Senior, C.P., S.T.D.

S **Sadlier Religion**

This advanced publication copy has been printed prior to final publication and pending ecclesiastical approval.

Acknowledgments

This publication was printed with permission pending from the following copyright holders.

Excerpts from the *Catechism of the Catholic Church, second edition,* © 2000, Libreria Editrice Vaticana—United States Conference of Catholic Bishops, Washington, D.C. All rights reserved.

Scripture texts in this work are taken from the *New American Bible, revised edition* © 2010, 1991, 1986, 1970 Confraternity of Christian Doctrine, Washington, D.C. All Rights Reserved. No part of the *New American Bible* may be reproduced in any form without permission in writing from the copyright owner.

Excerpts from the English translation of *The Roman Missal* © 2010 International Commission on English in the Liturgy, Inc. (ICEL). All rights reserved.

Excerpts from the English translation of *Rite of Penance* © 1974, International Committee on English in the Liturgy, Inc. All rights reserved.

Excerpts from *The Order of Confirmation.* Copyright © 2016, United States Conference of Catholic Bishops, Inc., Washington, D.C. All rights reserved.

Quotations from papal addresses, audiences, homilies, speeches, messages, meditations, encyclicals, and other Vatican documents are from www.vatican.va and copyright © by Libreria Editrice Vaticana.

English translation of the Glory to the Father, Apostles' Creed, Nicene Creed, and the Lord's Prayer by the International Consultation on English Texts (ICET).

Excerpts from *Catholic Household Blessings and Prayers (Revised Edition)* © 1988, 2007, United States Catholic Conference, Inc. Washington, D.C. All rights reserved.

Excerpts from the Web sites of the St. Peter Claver Society, the Diocese of St. Petersburg, Loyola Press, and the Sacred Hearts Community © 2018. All rights reserved.

Copyright © 2020 by William H. Sadlier, Inc. All rights reserved. This book, or any part thereof, may not be reproduced in any form, or by any means, including electronic, photographic, or mechanical, or by any sound recording system, or by any device for storage and retrieval of information, without the written permission of the publisher.

Printed in the United States of America.

S® and Sadlier Religion® are registered trademarks of William H. Sadlier, Inc. All rights reserved.

CHRIST IN US™ is a trademark of William H. Sadlier, Inc.

William H. Sadlier, Inc.
9 Pine Street
New York, NY 10005-4700

ISBN: 978-0-8215-3691-9

2 3 4 5 6 7 8 9 WEBC 23 22 21

Cover Series Design: Silver Linings Studios. **Cover Series Illustrator:** Jui Ishida.

Photo Credits

age fotostock/Spencer Grant: 71 *right*; Blend Images / KidStock: 38, 88; Blend Images/Sollina Images: 65; Juice Images: 182; SW Productions: 172; Wavebreak Media: 63. Alamy Stock Photo/vvvita: 123; Oksana Bratanova: 149; Linda Kennedy: 219; Aidan Melas: 56, 248 *bottom*; Myrleen Pearson: 242; Marmaduke St. John: 71 *top*, 73, 217; Blend Images/KidStock: 30; Blend Images/Jose Luis Pelaez Inc: 205; Borderlands: 54; Design Pics, Inc/Carson Ganci: 111; Godong: 64 *right*; graja: 74; Hero Images Inc.: 28; Pontino: 79. Bridgeman Images/Look and Learn/Private Collection: 23, 250; Mondadori/Electa/Luigi Baldin: 203 *bottom*. Karen Callaway: 24, 51, 164, 189, 191 *top*, 229. The Crosiers/Gene Plaisted, OSC: 46, 44, 72, 90, 97, 247, 249 *top*, 255. Dann Tardif Photography: 131. Dreamstime.com/Yelena Rodriguez: 153. Fotolia.com/alinamd: 178; Angelov: 169; daynamore: 156; Tomsickova: 116; YakobchukOlena: 104; Glenda Powers: 173; Monkey Business: 113. Getty Images/by mira: 87; laflor: 127; pamela_d_mcadams: 115; sedmak: 136; Westend61: 107; Yukmin: 35; Ghislain & Marie David de Lossy: 155; Pascal Deloche: 170; Sebastien Desarmaux: 81; Ed Freeman: 128; Ariel Skelley: 187; Ted Soqui: 180; Inti St Clair: 139; Con Tanasiuk: 124; Blend Images/John Lund: 52; Blend Images/Jose Luis Pelaez Inc: 37; Blend Images/Jose Luis Pelaez Inc: 162; Boston Globe/Jessica Rinaldi: 199; Choreograph: 93; Cravan Images: 129; Digital Vision: 121; FatCamera: 154; Hill Street Studios: 138; Jupiterimages: 31. Good Salt, Inc./Lars Justinen: 22; Justinen Creative: 150; Lifeway Collection: 86, 108, 147, 181; Providence Collection: 45, 47, 148; Review & Herald Publishing: 227 *bottom*; The Classic Bible Art Collection: 221 *bottom*. Greg Lord: 239. iStockphoto.com/aldomurillo: 158; asiseeit: 95; Cecilie_Arcurs: 165; CraigRJD: 174; debbiehelbing: 85; fstop123: 145; George Peters: 209 *top*; Georgy_Golovin: 232–233 *bottom*; Imgorthand: 122, 140; isitsharp: 96; Juanmonino: 157; kali9: 132, vii; Kenishirotie: 177; Kontrec: 94; mandygodbehear: 163; pixelfusion3d: 166; SaigeYves: 179; sankai: 218; sedmak: 197 *bottom*; shironosov: 55; tatyana_tomsickova: 135; valbar: 146; vgajic: 20; VikahSuh: 251; yipengge: 64 *left*; FatCamera: 231; monkeybusinessimages: 48, 130, 15; Morsa Images: 78; Rawpixel: 114, vi; SolStock: 32; Wavebreakmedia: 105. Ken Karp Photography Inc.: 171. Masterfile/Kevin Dodge: 40. Neal Farris: 29. Shutterstock.com/arapix: 12; atikinka: 207; buchan: 236, 237 *bottom*; ESB Professional: 11; irin-k: 190–191 *bottom*; Macrovector: 196–197 *top*, 202–203 *top*, 220–221 *top*, 226–227 *top*; MagicBones: 212; Redcollegiya: 190–191 *background*, 208–209 *background*, 214–215 *background*, 232–233 *background*, 235 *background*; Slanapotam: 18, 60, 102, 144, 186; SNEHIT: 230; unguryanu: 223, 252; Galyna Andrushko: 206; Felix-Andrei Constantinescu: 201; R. Daniluk: 21, 253; Nataliya Dolotko: 235; Joana Lopes: 43; Philip Meyer: 237 *top*; Oksana Mizina: 215 *top*; Renata Sedmakova: 225; Gordana Sermek: 208–209 *bottom*; Anna Subbotina: 214–215 *bottom*; Chollachart Tabtimngam: 224; Romolo Tavani: 256; Jiri Vaclavek: 200; Lawence Wee: 193; horizonphoto: 194; Ink Drop: 213; Monkey Business Images: 112; wavebreakmedia: 14, 98; WPixz: 188. Spirit Juice Studios: 61, 71 *left*, 71 *center left*, 77, 89, 233 *top*, 248 *center*. Stockbyte/George Doyle: 19, 69, 119. SuperStock/Blend Images/Mike Kemp: 106; Blend Images/Jon Feingersh: 211; Caia Images: 27; Exactostock: 161; Hemis.fr/Stephane Lemaire: 36; Hero Images Inc.: 195; Stockbroker: 103. W.P. Wittman Limited: 53, 62, 70, 71 *center*, 71 *center right*, 238, 248 *top*, 249 *bottom*.

Illustrator Credits

Alois di Leo: 36, 39, 42, 50, 134, 137, 152, 160, 168, 184, 194, 195, 201, 219, 225. Robert Kayganich: 240–241. Jim Madsen: 17, 59, 101, 143, 243, 244, 245, 246. David Sossella: 52, 55, 66, 80, 84. Christopher Thornock: 10, 13, 25, 33, 41, 49, 57, 67, 75, 83, 91, 99, 109, 117, 125, 133, 141, 151, 159, 167, 175, 183, 254.

Christ In Us was developed in collaboration with the wisdom of the community. The team included respected catechetical, liturgical, pastoral, and theological experts who shared their insights and inspired its development.

With grateful acknowledgment of
William Sadlier Dinger and Frank Sadlier Dinger
for their leadership, vision, and commitment to excellence in the development
of Sadlier's catechetical programs and resources since 1963

Theological and Liturgical Consultants

Most Reverend Christopher James Coyne
Bishop of Burlington, VT

Donna Eschenauer, Ph.D.
Associate Dean, Associate Professor of
    Pastoral Theology
St. Joseph's Seminary and College

Rita Ferrone, M.Div.

Thomas Kendzia
Sadlier National Consultant for
    Liturgy and Music

Reverend Monsignor John Pollard,
    M. Ed., ST.L.

Alissa Thorell, M.T.S

John B. Angotti, M.A.P.S.

Barbara Sutton, D.Min.

Kathleen Dorsey Bellow, D.Min.

Scripture Consultant

Reverend Donald Senior, C.P., S.T.D.
Chancellor and President Emeritus
    Catholic Theological Union

Catechetical Consultants

Amy Welborn, M.A.

Susan Stark

Sr. Theresa Engel, O.S.F.
Member of the School Sisters of St. Francis

Maureen A. Kelly, M.A.

Karla Manternach, M.A.

Woodeene Koenig-Bricker, M.A.

Connie Clark

Shannon Chisholm, Ph.D.

Susan M. Sink

Maureen Shaughnessy, S.C.

Lori Dahlhoff, Ed.D.

Andrea D. Chavez-Kopp, M.Ed.

Educational Consultants

Richard Culatta

Heidi Hayes Jacobs, Ed.D.

Jay McTighe

Allie Johnston

Learning Style Inclusion Consultants

Charleen Katra, M.A.

Jennifer Ochoa, M.Ed., LDT/C

Inculturation Consultants

Luis J. Medina
Director, Bilingual Catechesis

Charlene Howard, M.A.

Michael P. Howard, M.A.
Eat the Scroll Ministry

Catholic Social Teaching

Kristin Witte, D.Min.

Genevieve Jordan Laskey, M.A.

Michael Jordan Laskey, M.A.

Media and Technology Consultants

Spirit Juice Studios

Top Floor Productions

Sr. Caroline Cerveny, S.S.J.-T.O.S.F., D.Min.

Reviewers and Contributors

Jennifer Hayhurst

Concetta M. Duval, Ed.D.

Trenton W. Mattingly, M.A.

Debi Mahr, M.A.

Mary Homola, M.A.

Linda Mele Dougherty, M.A.

Mary Jane Krebbs, Ph.D.

Darcy Osby, M.Div.

Hugh M. Keenan

Sadlier Consultant Team

Steven Botsford
Senior Director of Digital Catechesis

Suzan Larroquette, M.T.S.
Senior Director of Catechetical Consultant Services

Kathleen Hendricks, M.A.
National Catechetical Consultant
  Contributing Writer

John Collins, M.Ed.
National Religion Consultant

Writing/Development Team

Diane Lampitt, M.Ed.
Vice President, Product Manager, Religion

Blake Bergen
Vice President, Religion Editorial

Deacon Matthew Halbach, Ph.D.
Senior Director of Catechesis

Regina Kelly, M.A.
Editorial Director, Religion

Gloria Shahin, M.A.
Senior Editorial Director, Religion

Mary Carol Kendzia, M.S.
Research and Development Director, Religion

Robert Vigneri, M.S.
Executive Editor, Religion

Editorial Staff
Tina Dennelly, Linda Nicholson, Roger Ochoa,
Amanda Pisciotta

Publishing Operations Team

Patricia Coryell
Senior Vice President & Publisher

Kevin Feyen
Vice President, Shared Services

Carole Uettwiller
Vice President, Supply Chain

Vince Gallo
Senior Creative Director

Francesca O'Malley
Art/Design Director

Cesar Llacuna
Senior Image Manager

Roderick Gammon
Senior Director, Digital Strategy

Toby Carson
Digital Design Director

Cheryl Golding
Senior Production Director

Laura Reischour
Project Manager

Evie Alvarez
Program Manager

Jovito Pagkalinawan
Electronic Prepress Director

Yolanda Miley
Image Rights & Permissions Director

Lucy Rotondi
Business Manager

Design/Image Staff
Kevin Butler, Nancy Figueiredo,
Stephen Flanagan, Debrah Kaiser,
Gabriel Ricci, Bob Schatz, Daniel Sherman

Production Staff
Robin D'Amato, Carol Lin, Vincent
McDonough, Allison Pagkalinawan,
Brad Tucker

Contents

Your Spiritual Journey

Christ In Us offers a saint for every grade. As you journey through each unit, remember to pray to your grade's saint. Ask him or her to help guide you to be closer to Jesus Christ.

Saint Francis of Assisi was born into a very wealthy family. He always had the best things money could buy. Francis also had a lot of friends. However, money and friends did not make him happy.

When Francis got older, he heard the voice of Christ. He started giving all his money and things to the poor. But Francis quickly realized that the best gift he could give to God was not money or things. It was the gift of his life.

This inspired Francis to live a life of poverty and serve the poor. Many of his friends even started to follow his example.

In his poverty, Francis began to see God in all of creation. It changed him! From then on, he spent his life caring for all of God's people, animals, and nature. Francis wrote a hymn in praise of creation.

Welcome to **Christ In Us**, an exciting way to grow in your Catholic faith!

Each one of us is on a journey to love and know Jesus Christ. Imagine if every person who met you knew you were a friend of Christ!

Together in this program, we will:
ENCOUNTER Jesus Christ
ACCOMPANY him in our lives
WITNESS to our faith.

You will use this book as well as your online digital portal as you discover and grow closer to Jesus Christ.

As you journey in your faith, you can think about these questions:

"It is Christ in you, the hope for glory."
Colossians 1:27

What would happen if you did not have Jesus in your life?

Why is it important to have Christ live in you?

How do your faith, the Church, and your family help bring you closer to God?

Every lesson has four **Spiraling Main Ideas.** Here is an example.

Faith Words in the lessons help you understand the important words we use as Catholics.

Be sure to look at all the wonderful photos and beautiful art in the pages of your book.

As you explore this question, you might be asked to stop and think more about it and then do a short **Activity** to answer it better.

You will be asked to **Show What You Know** by writing the answers to some short questions pertaining to the lesson.

The Church is the family of God.

Jesus is a part of our lives, just like our family and friends. Jesus is with us all the time. Jesus is with us in a very special way in the **Church**.

We become members of the Church at Baptism. The Church is the People of God throughout the world. God calls us together to be his people, the Church.

The Word of God and the Eucharist give the Church life. The Church is also called the Body of Christ. The Church is like a family that wants to know and love God together. The Church is the family of God. Jesus is the head of that family. He is always with the Church.

Jesus gave us the Church to tell us about and share his love for us. The Church also helps us share the love of the Blessed Trinity with others. We are blessed to be a part of the Church!

Faith Word

Church all the people who are baptized in the name of the Blessed Trinity and are part of the Body of Christ

Activity

The Church is like a family. Draw a picture of your family. Tell a friend about your drawing.

24 ACCOMPANY

You will not be alone as you journey through **Christ In Us**. You will have lots of **Partners in Faith**—saints and other holy people who lived amazing lives—walking with you.

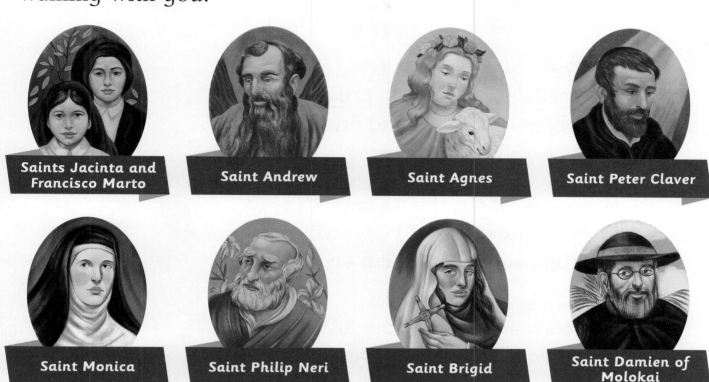

Saints Jacinta and Francisco Marto

Saint Andrew

Saint Agnes

Saint Peter Claver

Saint Monica

Saint Philip Neri

Saint Brigid

Saint Damien of Molokai

Next, you will be asked to go to your **Portfolio** to creatively share how you can bring Christ to the world.

Each lesson ends with a **Mini-Task** that invites you to show ways you can live out your faith as a missionary disciple of Christ.

Finally, you will be given ways to think and talk with your family **At Home**.

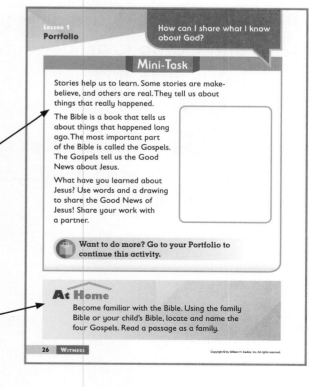

Lesson 1
Portfolio

How can I share what I know about God?

Mini-Task

Stories help us to learn. Some stories are make-believe, and others are real. They tell us about things that really happened.

The Bible is a book that tells us about things that happened long ago. The most important part of the Bible is called the Gospels. The Gospels tell us the Good News about Jesus.

What have you learned about Jesus? Use words and a drawing to share the Good News of Jesus! Share your work with a partner.

Want to do more? Go to your Portfolio to continue this activity.

At Home

Become familiar with the Bible. Using the family Bible or your child's Bible, locate and name the four Gospels. Read a passage as a family.

Copyright © by William H. Sadlier, Inc. All rights reserved.

Christic In Us features an online portal filled with exciting media and activities to go with the lessons in your book. If you see one of these icons below in your book, you know it's time to visit the student portal for more. (Note: Not every icon will appear in your book.)

 Participate in lesson prayers, whose words are online and downloadable.

Learn more about the lesson's **Did You Know?** topic by watching an interesting video and doing an activity.

 Learn more about the lesson's **Partner in Faith** by watching an online video and completing the activity that follows.

Listen to Scripture verses and Catholic prayers and learn them by heart.

 Find fun activities to share and recall what you have learned.

Show What You Know by completing online assessments.

Read and remember the **Faith Words** definitions.

Complete projects and tasks in the online **Portfolio** or *Portfolio Workbook*.

Listen to the songs for your grade level and sing along!

Your Songs for Grade 1	
Unit Songs	**Liturgical Catechesis Seasonal Songs**
Unit 1: "In My Heart," Spiritual	**Lent:** "Christ Be Our Light," Bernadette Farrell/OCP
Unit 2: "Light of Christ," Tom Kendzia,/OCP	**Church Year:** "Open My Eyes," Jesse Manibusan/OCP
Unit 3: "Prayer of St. Francis," Sebastian Temple/OCP	**Ordinary Time:** "Wade in the Water," Spiritual
Unit 4: "We Are Marching," African Traditional	**Triduum:** "Take Up Your Cross," Jaime Cortez/OCP
Unit 5: "We Will Praise You," Tom Kendzia/OCP	

Your journey continues with your login to *Christ In Us* Digital!

Here you can explore all the exciting resources that blend together with your textbook.

Take a look at your personalized online dashboard. Everything you need is at your fingertips!

- Think of your **Portfolio** as your digital backpack! Here you can get your assignments, see reminders, send emails, and even talk to your catechist.

- Interactive Mini-Tasks enable you to share exciting activities with others. You will be able to get hands on and creative by making videos or interactive posters.

- Listen with your heart and pray the prayers of *Lectio* and *Visio Divina*, praise, petition, intercession, adoration, and blessing from your lesson.

- Track your progress with digital quizzes, medals, and tests.

Have a wonderful year!

Unit 1
The Faith Professed

The Nativity

Unit Prayer

Leader: Saint Francis of Assisi found God in all of creation. Not only in the beauty of all the earth, but also in each of us, our families, and everyone on earth.

Let us listen to how God's love is made known to us today.

Let us pray:
O God, we praise and thank you for the beauty in all of creation.

All: We praise you, O Lord, for your great love.

Leader: For our families' love for us,

All: we praise you, O Lord, for your great love.

Leader: For creating us in your image,

All: we praise you, O Lord, for your great love.

Leader: For the gift of the Church to us and the world,

All: we praise you, O Lord, for your great love.

All sing: "In My Heart"

 Unit Song: "In My Heart," **Spiritual**

Missionary Discipleship

How does your family, a friend, or a pet help you know how much God loves you? In what ways do you celebrate God's love for you?

How do we know God?

Do you know why you are learning about your Catholic faith? Your family wants you to come to know God! God made us. God loves us. He knows you and every person by name. God wants us to know and love him, too.

How do we know God? He gave us many ways to know him. The Bible and the Church tell us about God's love. Jesus shows us the most how much God loves us.

Go to the digital portal for a prayer of blessing.

"Everything God created is good."
1 Timothy 4:4

God always loves us.

God made the whole world. God made every person in the world. God made you, too! Everything God made tells us about his love.

God made people to share in his love. God knows everything about us. God knows when we are happy or sad. God cares about us when we are sick. God even knows how many hairs are on our heads!

God promises to love us forever. God loves us always, no matter what.

God wants us to love him, too!

In what ways can I tell that someone loves me?

Did You Know?

 God shares his love through stories.

The Bible tells us about God's love.

God wants all people to know about his love for us. One way God tells us about his love is in the **Bible**.

The Bible was written by people very long ago. But the Bible is God's own Word to us. God inspired the people who wrote it. Through their writing, he shared what he wants us to know about him.

The Bible teaches us about God's love. We read the Bible to learn more about God.

Faith Word

Bible the Church's holy book of God's Word

Activity

Who teaches you about God? Draw a picture of one person who teaches you about God's love.

God the Father sent his Son, Jesus.

We pray: "In the name of the Father, and of the Son, and of the Holy Spirit." The Bible tells us that God the Father sent his Son, Jesus, to us. Jesus showed us how much God loves us.

Jesus is the Son of God. Jesus is God. Jesus loves us.

The Bible tells us many things about Jesus. He taught his followers how to pray. He helped and healed people. He showed love for all people.

Jesus is God the Son.

God the Son was born to Mary in Bethlehem and was named Jesus. He is and always was and always will be God, but he is also truly man. Everything Jesus said or did showed his love for us.

The Church is the family of God.

Jesus is a part of our lives, just like our family and friends. Jesus is with us all the time. Jesus is with us in a very special way in the **Church**.

We become members of the Church at Baptism. The Church is the People of God throughout the world. God calls us together to be his people, the Church.

The Word of God and the Eucharist give the Church life. The Church is also called the Body of Christ. The Church is like a family that wants to know and love God together. The Church is the family of God. Jesus is the head of that family. He is always with the Church.

Jesus gave us the Church to tell us about and share his love for us. The Church also helps us share the love of the Blessed Trinity with others. We are blessed to be a part of the Church!

Faith Word

Church all the people who are baptized in the name of the Blessed Trinity and are part of the Body of Christ

Activity

The Church is like a family. Draw a picture of your family. Tell a friend about your drawing.

Faith Words

Bible   **Church**

 Show What You Know

Circle the word that answers each question.

1. Who is the Son of God?

Jesus | Joseph

2. What is the Bible?

God's Word | a picture book

3. Trace the word to finish the sentence. Jesus is always with us. He is with us in a special way in the

Church .

Partners in Faith
Saint Francis of Assisi

Saint Francis of Assisi loved all of God's creation. He wants us to love it, too. He thanked God for all of creation.

 Learn more about the life of Saint Francis of Assisi.

Copyright © by William H. Sadlier, Inc. All rights reserved.

How can I share what I know about God?

Mini-Task

Stories help us to learn. Some stories are make-believe, and others are real. They tell us about things that really happened.

The Bible is a book that tells us about things that happened long ago. The most important part of the Bible is called the Gospels. The Gospels tell us the Good News about Jesus.

What have you learned about Jesus? Use words and a drawing to share the Good News of Jesus! Share your work with a partner.

 Want to do more? Go to your Portfolio to continue this activity.

At Home

Become familiar with the Bible. Using the family Bible or your child's Bible, locate and name the four Gospels. Read a passage as a family.

Copyright © by William H. Sadlier, Inc. All rights reserved.

Who is God?

God made us to show his love for us. He created us to know him, to love him, and to serve him. God takes care of us. He takes care of the whole world.

God is always with us. God the Father sent his Son. Jesus is the Son of God. God the Father and Jesus sent the Holy Spirit. God the Father, the Son, and the Holy Spirit are at work in the world together.

Go to the digital portal for a traditional prayer.

"Blessed are you, Lord God of all creation."
Roman Missal

God cares for all of creation.

God made everything. The word *create* means "to make." **Creation** is everything God made out of nothing. He made you, too.

Faith Word

creation
everything God made out of nothing

God made your heart beat and your lungs ready to breathe. God made everything without any help at all. The Bible tells us: "God looked at everything he had made, and found it very good" (Genesis 1:31).

God is still at work in creation. He makes the sun rise and set. God makes the rivers flow. He helps you learn and grow. God always cares for the world he made!

What are some ways that God shows his love for me?

Did You Know?

 Signs are all around us.

God the Father, God the Son, and God the Holy Spirit are the Blessed Trinity. They are One God in Three Persons.

We know that God made us. But who made God?

No one made him. Even when there was nothing else, God already was. God always will be. He is forever. That is longer than we can even imagine!

There is only One God, but God is also Three Persons. God is Father, Son, and Holy Spirit. We know this because God told us. We call God the **Blessed Trinity**. We pray to the Blessed Trinity "in the name of the Father, and of the Son, and of the Holy Spirit."

Faith Word

Blessed Trinity One God in Three Persons: God the Father, God the Son, and God the Holy Spirit

 The Sign of the Cross

Tri- is a word part that means "three." A tricycle is a bike with three wheels. *Tri-* is also in *Trinity*. The Blessed Trinity is One God in Three Persons.

God is One. God the Father, God the Son, and God the Holy Spirit are one in love. The Blessed Trinity is not made of different parts. God is not made of parts.

We can never fully understand the mystery of the Trinity.

Activity

Sometimes a shamrock is used as a symbol of the Blessed Trinity. The leaf of a shamrock has three parts, but it is one leaf. Draw a shamrock and color it. Then complete the sentence.

The Blessed Trinity is Three Persons in One

Jesus is God's only Son and our Lord.

Jesus is God himself. Jesus is the Second Person of the Blessed Trinity. He is both fully God and fully man. Jesus is the only Son of God.

We also call Jesus "Lord." The name *Lord* shows that we know that Jesus is God. It means we believe in Jesus. We worship only God. We worship Jesus because he is God.

Jesus is present in the Church by the power of the Holy Spirit.

God the Father sent us his Son, Jesus. This shows the Father's great love for us. God sends us the Holy Spirit, too. God the Father, God the Son, and God the Holy Spirit are at work in the world together.

Through the power of the Holy Spirit, Jesus is present with the Church. The Church is sometimes described as a boat. The people who believe in Jesus, are baptized, and follow his teachings are in the boat with Jesus.

Jesus shows us which way to sail. The Holy Spirit is like the wind that fills the sail and directs the boat. Jesus and the Holy Spirit are always with the Church. They work together to make the Church unified and holy.

Activity

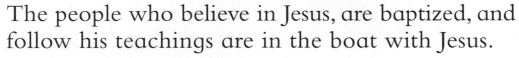

Draw a picture of a boat. The boat is a symbol for the Church. Put Jesus and your family in the boat. Draw the Holy Spirit like the wind. Draw where the boat is going. Why is the boat going to this place?

Faith Words

creation   **Blessed Trinity**

 Show What You Know

Trace the words to finish the sentences.

1. _____Creation_____ is everything God made.

2. The Blessed Trinity is God the Father, God the Son,

   and God the _____Holy_____ Spirit.

Circle the correct answer.

3. God the Father, God the Son, and God the Holy
   Spirit are One God in Three _____ .

   Persons | Parts

Partners in Faith

Saint Martin de Porres

Saint Martin de Porres helped people who were poor and sick. He gave all his time to caring for others. He asks us to take care of each other.

 Learn more about the life of Saint Martin de Porres.

Copyright © by William H. Sadlier, Inc. All rights reserved.

Mini-Task

In this lesson, you learned that God is always with us. We can see signs of God's love all around us. Creation can show us God's love. Family and friends can show us God's love.

Draw someone or something from your life that reminds you how much God loves you.

Tell a partner about your drawing.

Ask your partner to tell you about his or her drawing.

 Want to do more? Go to your Portfolio to continue this activity.

At Home

See God's love in creation by playing a game of I Spy. Point out things that God has made as you walk through your neighborhood.

Copyright © by William H. Sadlier, Inc. All rights reserved.

Why did God make us?

God made us to share in his life and love. He made us to live together in happiness. He wants us to love one another. God wants us to love him, too. God wants us to be close to him forever.

God gives us the gift of faith. Faith helps us to believe in God and the truth he has told us about himself. The Church helps us believe in God, too. The Church helps us to live as God's children.

 Go to the digital portal for a prayer of praise.

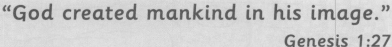

"God created mankind in his image."
Genesis 1:27

God created everything.

God made every living thing out of nothing. He made birds that fly, fish that swim, and animals that crawl on land. Everything God has made shows us his goodness and beauty.

Of all living things, God made each person in his own image. God shares his goodness and beauty with human beings in a special way.

What is my favorite part of God's creation?

Did You Know?

The Church has a special care for God's creation.

Activity

God created the world. Look carefully at the picture. Color all the living things God has created. Talk about your picture with a friend.

God's gift of faith helps us believe in him and obey him.

God loves us very much. He made us to love as he does. God wants us to love him and to love one another.

Our hearts want God more than anything. Deep inside us, we know that nothing can make us happier than God.

No other living thing knows that God made it. Only human beings know God and have **faith**. Faith is a gift from God that helps us to trust him and believe in him. Faith helps us obey and do what God wants us to do. It helps us believe in God even though we cannot know or understand everything about him. God gave the gift of faith only to human beings.

Faith Word

faith a gift from God that helps us to believe in him

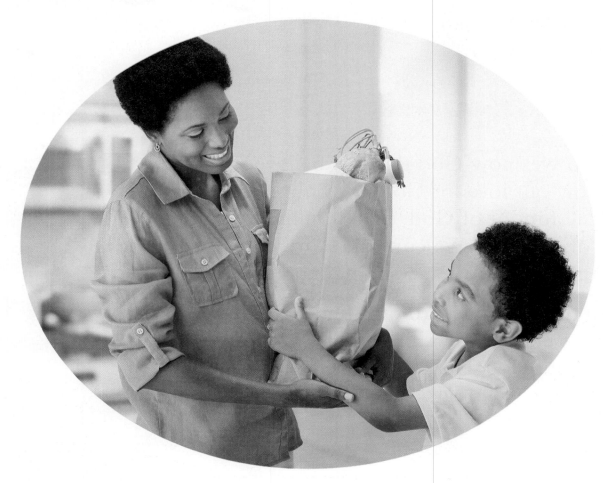

How do we show God that we believe in him? We can show our love for God first by praying, especially with the family of God, the Church. We can also learn about God. We can take care of the world he gave us, and love the people he made.

We do these things with our family. We also do these things as part of the Church. The Church helps us learn about God. The Church helps our faith in God grow strong. The Church helps us to do what God asks us to do.

God tells us how to live.

God made us to live together and to love one another. God made us good. He made us to do good things. But sometimes we do things that are not good.

The Bible tells us about Adam and Eve, the first people that God made. God wanted them to live as his children. He gave them rules to follow. He wanted them to be good.

God did not force them to follow his rules. He let them choose for themselves. But they did not obey him.

God tells us how to live. The Church helps us to know what God wants from us. Then God lets us choose. Do we choose to live as his children? Do we do the things God wants us to do?

God made us to be his children. He wants us to show our love for him. We act like God's children when we are kind to others.

Activity

Circle the differences between the two drawings. Color the child who is doing what God wants.

God wants us to live as his children forever.

The Bible tells us that "whoever does what is good is of God" (3 John 1:11). That means that when we do good, we are the way God wants us to be. We share in his goodness.

God made us very good. He wants us to be close to him and to be kind to others. When we disobey God's laws, he always gives us another chance. God wants us to keep trying to be good.

God wants us to live with him forever. When we live as God's children now, we show him that we want to live as his children forever!

Activity

Complete the sentences. Use the words below.

good **children**

God wants us to be _____ .

God wants us to live as his _____ .

Faith Word

faith

 Show What You Know

Put a check mark next to the correct answer.

1. This is a gift from God that helps us believe in him and trust him.

   ☐ rules   ☐ faith

2. When we have faith and obey God, we can live with him _____.

   ☐ forever   ☐ for today

Circle the things God wants us to be.

3. good   angry   his children   sad

Partners in Faith

Saints Jacinta and Francisco Marto

Jacinta and Francisco were children who lived in Fatima, Portugal. They saw Mary, Jesus' mother. She asked them to pray to ask God to help the world. They had faith in God and did what Mary asked. They teach us to pray, too.

 Learn more about the lives of Saints Jacinta and Francisco Marto.

Copyright © by William H. Sadlier, Inc. All rights reserved.

How can I show that I am a child of God?

Mini-Task

Living as a child of God means loving others.

Look closely at the picture.

What is happening in this picture? Think aloud with a partner.

Circle the child in the picture who is showing the most love for others.

 Want to do more? Go to your Portfolio to continue this activity.

At Home

Talk about things that last a long time. How can you help each other understand that God's love is forever?

Copyright © by William H. Sadlier, Inc. All rights reserved.

Who is Jesus Christ?

Jesus Christ is the Son of God. Jesus is God's greatest gift to us. We call Jesus "Christ" because he was sent by God the Father. Jesus is always with us in the Church. Jesus lives with the Father and the Holy Spirit in heaven. He wants us to live in heaven forever, too.

 Go to the digital portal for a _Lectio_ and _Visio Divina_ prayer.

 "God so loved the world that he gave his only Son." John 3:16

God chose Mary to be the mother of Jesus.

God sent an **angel** to Mary. Angels are special beings who serve God forever. The angel told Mary that God chose her to be the mother of his Son. The angel told Mary to name her Son Jesus.

Mary did not understand how she could give birth to God's Son. But Mary loved God and trusted him. She wanted to serve him. She was willing to do whatever God asked. Mary said "yes" to God!

God sent the Holy Spirit to Mary. The Holy Spirit remained in her and helped prepare her to be Jesus' mother. We call Mary the Mother of God because she gave birth to Jesus, and Jesus is God. We are blessed that God chose Mary. We are blessed that Mary said "yes" to God! Mary is truly the Mother of God.

Faith Word

angel an invisible being that is a messenger of God

AVE·GRATIA PLENA·DOMINUS·TECUM.

In what ways can I show God that I want to do what he asks of me?

 Guardian Angel Prayer

Did You Know?

 Mary is our model.

The Bible tells us that Mary was away from home when Jesus was born. Jesus was born in a stable. It was the only place Mary and her husband, Joseph, could find to rest.

Mary and Joseph named the newborn child "Jesus," as the angel had said. The name *Jesus* means "God saves." Mary took care of Jesus the same way someone took care of you when you were born. She held Jesus. She fed him. She kept him warm.

 Hail Mary

Activity

We are blessed that Mary said "yes" to God. Draw a thank-you card to Mary. Explain to a friend why you are thankful that Mary said "yes."

Jesus is God's only Son.

Jesus is the Second Person of the Blessed Trinity. God the Father sent God the Son, Jesus. This happened by the power of God the Holy Spirit.

The Son of God came to live with us. He became like you and me. But he was still God. Jesus was God the Father's only Son. There have been many people in the world, but Jesus is the only Son of God.

We also call Jesus the name **Christ**. *Christ* is a word that means "the anointed one" or "the chosen one of God." God sent us Jesus Christ to save us. Jesus is part of God's promise to love us always.

Jesus gives us new life.

Jesus shows us that we can live with God forever. Jesus came to give us new life with God. The Bible tells us that Jesus said:

> "I came so that they might have life" (John 10:10).

In Jesus, God came to live with us as a person like us. People are special to God! The birth of Jesus shows how much God loves us.

Jesus lived in our world for about thirty-three years. He helped and healed people. He forgave those who had disobeyed God's laws. He taught others about God and how to be happy with him forever.

Jesus gave his life for us. He died on the Cross out of love for us. He rose from the dead. Now he lives forever with his Father and the Holy Spirit. All these things were part of God's plan for us. He sent Jesus out of love for us.

Jesus lives with his Father and the Holy Spirit in heaven.

After he rose from the dead, Jesus returned to his Father. Jesus lives with God the Father and God the Holy Spirit in **heaven**. Heaven is life forever with God.

Faith Word

heaven life with God forever

Think about something that makes you very happy. God wants us to be even happier than that. God wants us to be happier than we can imagine. He wants us to live with him forever in heaven. Jesus shows us that we can!

Activity

What do you think heaven is like? Draw a picture. Put Jesus in the picture. Make sure you are in the picture, too!

Faith Words

| angel | Christ | heaven |

 Show What You Know

Trace the words to complete the sentences.

1. _____ Mary _____ is the mother of Jesus.

2. An _____ angel _____ told Mary that God wanted her to be the mother of his Son.

Circle the correct answer.

3. _____ is happiness with God forever.

Heaven | Home

Partners in Faith

Mary, Mother of God

God chose Mary to be the mother of Jesus. Mary is our mother, too. When we need help, we can pray to Mary. When we pray to Mary, we are asking her to talk to Jesus for us.

 Learn more about the life of Mary, Mother of God.

Copyright © by William H. Sadlier, Inc. All rights reserved.

How can I show my love for Jesus Christ?

Mini-Task

Listening to a person's words can tell us about his or her feelings. But we can also learn about a person's feelings by looking at his or her face. A person who is frowning may feel sad. A person who is smiling may feel joyful.

How does God's love make you feel? Make your face show that feeling. Now draw a picture of your face when you think about God's love for you.

Ask a partner to name the feeling in your drawing.

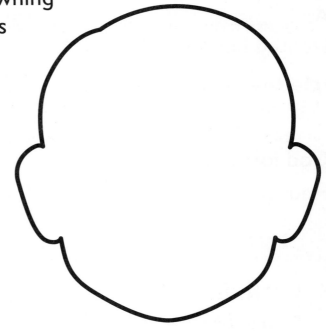

 Want to do more? Go to your Portfolio to continue this activity.

At Home

Remember that Mary was the mother of Jesus. Talk about ways your family prays to and honors Mary. How does Mary help your family say "yes" to God?

Copyright © by William H. Sadlier, Inc. All rights reserved.

What is the Church?

Jesus loves us. He wants us to believe in him and to follow him. Jesus gives us the Church to help us.

God gathers all his people together in the Church. The Holy Spirit guides the Church and makes the Church holy. The Church helps make our faith strong. Jesus invites everyone to the Church!

Go to the digital portal for a prayer of intercession.

"The Church is the People that God gathers in the whole world."
Catechism of the Catholic Church, 752

The Church is the People of God.

The word *church* with a small c is a building where we pray. *Church* with a capital C is the **People of God**. There are many church buildings, but there is only one Church. The People of God are baptized, believe in Jesus, and follow him. We grow in holiness together.

God created all people, all around the world. We speak different languages. We eat different foods. We live in different kinds of homes. But no matter how different we are, in the Church we are one family. Jesus is the head of the family.

The Church is One, just like the Blessed Trinity is One. The Church is united by the Holy Spirit. She is united in her faith in Jesus Christ.

Faith Word

People of God another name for the Church

How am I different from others? How am I the same?

Did You Know?

 The early Christians first worshiped at home.

Activity

God's people live all over the world. Look at the map. Color all the places where God's people live. Put an X where you live.

The Church is holy.

God himself gathers his people into the Church. Everything God does is holy. The Church is holy, too.

The Church helps us remember what Jesus taught us. The Church helps us know and understand Jesus' teaching. She guides us in being his followers. The Church helps us to do what God wants us to do.

The Church helps us to be holy. The Church is part of God's plan for us. What is one way the Church helps you to be holy?

The Holy Spirit guides the Church.

Jesus promised to send the Holy Spirit to his followers. Jesus kept his promise. The Holy Spirit helped the Church grow. The Holy Spirit guides the Church to do God's work in the world. He helps the Church carry out the mission, or special job, that Jesus gave her.

Some people in the world do not know God. Some do not have faith in him. But God loves all people. He wants all people to be close to him. With the help of the Holy Spirit, the Church shares God's love with the world.

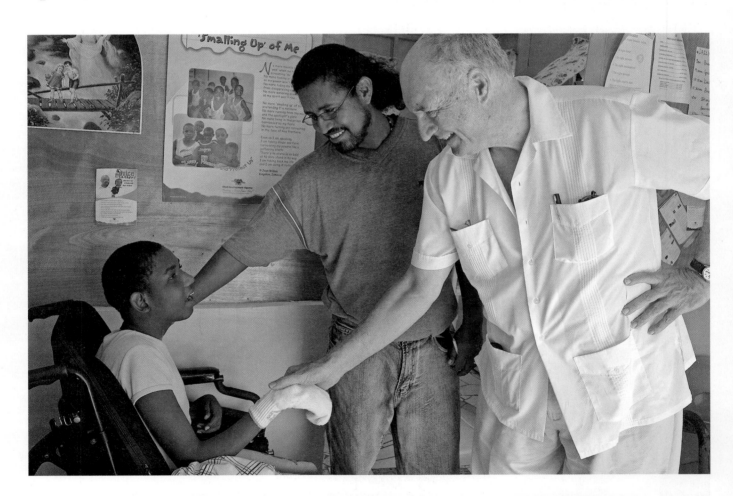

"Go into the whole world and proclaim the gospel to every creature."

Mark 16:15

The Holy Spirit helps the Church to tell others about Jesus. The Holy Spirit also helps us to remember the things that Jesus said and did. The Holy Spirit helps us tell others about Jesus and his Church.

The Holy Spirit gives us special gifts to help us know God. The Holy Spirit helps us understand what God asks of us. The Holy Spirit helps us bravely do what is right. The Holy Spirit is always with us!

Activity

The Holy Spirit helps us know Jesus. Unscramble this sentence to remember something about Jesus.

Son is the of Jesus God

_____

Jesus chose the Apostles to lead and care for the Church.

Before Jesus went to heaven, he chose twelve men to lead his followers. They were his **Apostles**. Jesus asked the Apostles to tell other people about him. After Jesus returned to his Father in heaven, the Apostles taught in his name. They taught about Jesus and his love. The Apostles spread the word about Jesus in many places.

The Church still does the work of the Apostles today. **Bishops, priests,** and **deacons** serve the Church, the People of God. Today, bishops continue the work of the Apostles. They lead the Church. Priests and deacons serve the Church by caring for God's people and leading them in prayer and worship.

Bishops, priests, and deacons teach us about God. With the help of the Holy Spirit, they help us understand who God is and what he wants us to know.

You can help do the work of the Church, too! You can tell people about God's love.

Faith Words

Apostles twelve men Jesus chose to lead his followers

bishops leaders of the Church who continue the work of the Apostles

priests men who serve the Church by teaching and leading our prayers

deacons men who serve the Church by assisting priests and bishops

Faith Words

| People of God | Apostles |
| priests | deacons | bishops |

 Show What You Know

Draw a circle around the correct answers.

1. The Church is the _____ .

People of God | deacons

2. _____ continue the work of the Apostles.

Angels | Bishops

Trace the word for the twelve men Jesus chose to lead his followers.

3. _____ Apostles _____

Partners in Faith
Saint Andrew

Saint Andrew was a fisherman. His brother was Saint Peter. When Andrew met Jesus, he became his follower. He was one of the first Apostles.

 Learn more about the life of Saint Andrew.

Copyright © by William H. Sadlier, Inc. All rights reserved.

Who helps guide me as a member of the Church?

Mini-Task

Priests and deacons teach us about God.

Who is the priest or deacon at your family's church?

My priest or deacon is named _____ .

Imagine that you will ask your priest or deacon a question.

Think about some questions you would like to ask.

Decide on one question you would like to ask the priest or deacon. Write it below.

_____

_____

_____

Want to do more? Go to your Portfolio to continue this activity.

At Home

After Mass on Sunday, talk about the difference between the church as a building and the Church as the People of God.

Copyright © by William H. Sadlier, Inc. All rights reserved.

How do we celebrate what we believe?

Mary and Elizabeth

Unit Prayer

Leader: Saint Francis of Assisi prayed: "Lord, make me an instrument of your peace. Where there is hatred, let me bring love."

Let us listen to how God's love is celebrated today. Listen to the stories of missionary disciples among us.

Let us pray:
O God, with Saint Francis we pray with his words: "Where there is hatred, let me bring love."

All: Lord, make me an instrument of your peace.

Leader: Grant that I may forgive others, try to understand others, and love my brothers and sisters.

All: Lord, make me an instrument of your peace.

Leader: With Saint Francis of Assisi, we pray: "Lord, make me an instrument of your peace."

All: Lord, make me an instrument of your peace.

All sing: "Light of Christ"

 Unit Song: "Light of Christ," Tom Kendzia/OCP

Missionary Discipleship

Jesus commanded us to love one another as he has loved us. How do the words Saint Francis prayed help us to live this command? When have you shown love by caring for another person?

How does God share his life with us?

Jesus gave us the Church. Jesus is present in the Church through the Holy Spirit. Jesus also gave us the sacraments. Through the sacraments, we share in God's own life. As the Church, we celebrate what we believe together.

Go to the digital portal for a prayer of blessing.

"Now you are Christ's body."
1 Corinthians 12:27

The Church continues Jesus' work of salvation.

The Church is the Body of Christ. Jesus Christ is the Head of the Church. Through the Church, Jesus continues his saving work in the world. He calls all people to be with him.

Faith Word

prayer listening to and talking with God

The Church prays together. **Prayer** is listening to and talking with God. When we pray with the Church, we pray with all believers, even those who are in heaven.

When the Church prays, believes, and celebrates, we are together with Jesus. We do not just think about Jesus. We do not just remember Jesus. We are actually *with* Jesus.

Who prays with me at church?

Did You Know?

 Catholics are praying every day throughout the world.

Jesus wants us to be with him always. He wants us to be with him now, and he wants us to have eternal life with the Blessed Trinity. *Eternal life* means "life forever."

 "God gave us eternal life, and this life is in his Son."

1 John 5:11

When we gather to be with Jesus now, we show that we want to be with God forever.

The Father, Jesus, and the Holy Spirit work together in the liturgy.

Liturgy is how the Church celebrates what we believe. Liturgy is the work and prayer of the whole Church.

The Blessed Trinity is present in the liturgy. In the liturgy, we pray to God the Father.

The Holy Spirit opens our hearts to Jesus. He helps us to listen and pay attention. He helps us know and understand what Jesus wants us to do.

The Holy Spirit prepares us to meet Jesus. Jesus is always with us in the liturgy. He is with us in the readings from the Bible. He is with us when the priest says and does what Jesus did. Jesus is especially with us in the Eucharist.

Faith Word

liturgy the work and prayer of the whole Church

Activity

Match the word to the picture. Then use the words in a sentence. Tell a friend how these things help us know that Jesus is with us always.

prayer

liturgy

Jesus gave the Church the sacraments.

The Father, Jesus, and the Holy Spirit work together in the Church. With Jesus and the Holy Spirit, the Church gives thanks and praise to God the Father.

Jesus also gave the Church the **sacraments**. The sacraments are special signs that help us share in God's life.

Faith Word

sacraments
special signs Jesus gave to the Church to share God's life and love with us

We gather as a Church community to celebrate the sacraments. The sacraments make us part of God's family. They strengthen our faith and help us grow in holiness.

Jesus wants us to have eternal life with the Blessed Trinity. He gave us the sacraments so that we could grow in holiness. Through the sacraments, Jesus chooses us and blesses us. Jesus brings us together and heals us.

Sacramentals are special prayers, actions, and objects.

Look around the next time you are at church. You might see a cross or special pictures or statues.

Sometimes we use objects like these to help us to pray. We call these objects **sacramentals**. Sacramentals are special blessings, prayers, actions, and objects. When a priest says a blessing over someone, that is a sacramental. When you bless yourself with holy water, that is a sacramental, too.

The Church gives us sacramentals to help us live a holy life. Being holy means being like Jesus. The Church uses sacramentals to help prepare us for the sacraments. Sacramentals also remind us to live as God's children every day, not just when we go to church.

Faith Word

sacramentals
blessings, actions, and objects that help us live holy lives

Activity

A rosary is a sacramental. We use it to honor Mary. Fill in the missing beads. Say a Hail Mary on each bead you draw. Color the whole rosary.

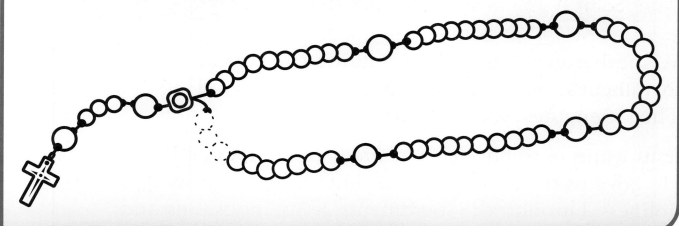

Faith Words

prayer	liturgy
sacraments	sacramentals

 ## Show What You Know

Put a check mark next to the correct answer.

1. _____ means listening to and talking with God.

   ☐ Prayer   ☐ Sacraments

2. Jesus gave us the _____ to share God's life with us.

   ☐ sacraments   ☐ rosary

3. _____ are special blessings, prayers, actions, and objects that help us live holy lives.

   ☐ Sacramentals   ☐ Liturgies

Partners in Faith

Saint Agnes

Saint Agnes was beautiful. People admired her for her beauty. But her faith and love for Jesus were most important to her. We honor her for her faithfulness to Jesus.

 Learn more about the life of Saint Agnes.

Copyright © by William H. Sadlier, Inc. All rights reserved.

How am I with Jesus?

Mini-Task

Prayer is listening to or talking with God.

We pray with the Church during Mass. We pray with our families at bedtime and at meals or other times of the day. We can also pray on our own any time. We can tell God anything when we pray.

Choose a time each day to talk with God.

Draw or write when you will pray each day.

What will you say to God?

_____

Try to remember to pray at this time each day.

 Want to do more? Go to your Portfolio to continue this activity.

At Home

With your family, talk about sacraments that people in your family have celebrated.

Copyright © by William H. Sadlier, Inc. All rights reserved.

How do we praise and thank God?

Jesus asked his followers to remember him. He asked the Apostles to teach the whole world about him. The Apostles taught people about Jesus and how to pray. Today, the Church still prays the way the Apostles taught us. We praise and thank God all year long. We do this in a special way on Sundays.

 Go to the digital portal for a _Lectio_ and _Visio Divina_ prayer.

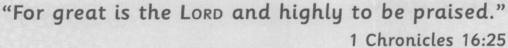

"For great is the LORD and highly to be praised."
1 Chronicles 16:25

We praise God every Sunday at Mass.

Faith Word

Mass the Church's most important celebration

Every Sunday is special in the Church. We call Sunday the Lord's Day. Jesus rose from the dead on a Sunday, the first Easter Sunday. The Lord's Day begins on Saturday evening and ends on Sunday evening. On the Lord's Day, the Church gathers to celebrate the **Mass**.

The Mass is the Church's most important celebration. Jesus is with us in a special way at Mass. He is with us in God's Word, in the person of the priest, and in the people. He is with us in a special way in the Eucharist, or Holy Communion. A priest always leads the people in celebrating the Mass.

At Mass, we praise God by singing and praying. We listen to God's Word. Jesus is with us in the Eucharist. We are sent out to share God's love with others.

In what ways do I participate at Mass?

Did You Know?

 Sunday is the first day of the week.

Usually, we celebrate the Mass with our **parish**. A parish is a community within the Church. The people in a parish **worship** God together. All over the world, the People of God gather with their parish on the Lord's Day. They gather to praise and worship God in the Mass.

Faith Words

parish a community within the Church that worships God together

worship adoration and honor given to God in prayer

Activity

Circle the actions you do at Mass to praise God. Choose one action to do better next week. Put a check mark next to it.

Ask the rest of your group which action they chose to do better.

We honor Mary and the saints all through the Church year.

The Church praises and thanks God throughout the year. We praise God in the liturgy, especially the Mass. During the Church year, we also remember holy events and people, such as **saints**.

We worship only God the Father, God the Son, and God the Holy Spirit. We honor Mary, the Mother of God. We honor the saints. They show us how to follow Jesus. We even ask the saints to pray for us, just as we might ask a friend to pray for us. Mary and the saints show us how to be holy.

Faith Word

saints followers of Jesus who led holy lives and now live happily forever with God in heaven

Activity

Complete the sentences. If you do not have a saint's name, choose a saint you would like to know more about.

I am named for Saint

_____.

His or her feast day is

_____.

Draw a picture of your name saint or a saint you want to learn more about.

Share your work with your group.

The Church shares Jesus' love and life in many ways.

Jesus asked the Apostles to help grow his Church. He asked them to remember him and to teach others about him. The Apostles worshiped God together. They taught others to worship him, too. Today, the Church shares Jesus' life and love in the Mass, the sacraments, and many other ways.

The Church celebrates certain seasons of the year. Each season, we remember something important about Jesus. We remember his birth and the time of waiting before he was born at Christmas. We remember the time Jesus spent with his followers. During the Easter season, we remember when Jesus died, rose, and went to live with his Father in heaven.

The Church remembers Jesus as the Apostles did before us. We may pray the Mass in different places, but we are one Church. We all pray as Jesus taught us.

Blessings and devotions are special prayers and actions.

There are many ways to pray. We can pray by ourselves or with others. We can learn the prayers of the Church or pray in our own words. We can praise God. We can thank God for his love. We can tell God we are sorry for something we did wrong. We can ask God for what we need.

The Church prays in the liturgy. The Church also praises and thanks God with blessings and devotions. **Blessings** praise God and remember all the good things he has done for us. Blessings also ask God to make someone or something holy. We can ask God to bless the people in our lives. We can also ask God to bless the things that happen in our lives.

Devotions help us worship God. They spread the good news of his love. They are a way to express our faith. Blessings and devotions are prayers. They show God that we love him. They help make our faith strong.

Faith Words

blessing a prayer that asks God to make someone or something holy

devotion a form of personal or communal prayer

Faith Words

Mass	parish	saints
blessing	devotion	worship

 Show What You Know

Circle the correct answer.

1. A _____ is a community within the Church that worships God together.

   parish | blessing

2. People who led holy lives and now live happily forever with God in heaven are called _____ .

   devotions | saints

Write the answer to the question.

3. What is the Church's most important celebration?

   _____

Partners in Faith
Saint Thomas

Saint Thomas the Apostle did not believe Jesus had risen. He doubted. Jesus showed his wounds to Thomas. Thomas then understood that Jesus was God.

 Learn more about the life of Saint Thomas.

Copyright © by William H. Sadlier, Inc. All rights reserved.

What helps me to praise and thank God?

Mini-Task

Turn and talk to a partner about the ways you praise and thank God.

Write one way that you praise or thank God.

Draw or design a Praise Card. It should show others a way to thank and praise God.

Share your card with a partner.

PRAISE GOD

 Want to do more? Go to your Portfolio to continue this activity.

 At Home

Sunday is a special day. Talk about Sunday with your family. What does your family do to honor it as the Lord's Day?

Copyright © by William H. Sadlier, Inc. All rights reserved.

How do we become members of the Church?

Jesus gave us the sacraments so that we could share in God's life. Three sacraments mark our belonging to the Church: Baptism, Confirmation, and the Eucharist. Our union with the Church begins at Baptism. Our membership in the Church is made complete in Confirmation and the Eucharist. These three sacraments are called the Sacraments of Christian Initiation. They help us follow Jesus and live as his followers.

Go to the digital portal for a prayer of thanksgiving.

"Now you are God's people."
1 Peter 2:10

Baptism, Confirmation, and the Eucharist make us members of the Church.

The Church celebrates seven sacraments. The sacraments help us grow closer to God. They help us to follow Jesus.

There are three sacraments that together make us members of the Church. These are the Sacraments of Initiation. They are Baptism, Confirmation, and the Eucharist. In some parishes, people receive all three of these sacraments at the same time. In other places, people receive them at different times of their lives.

Together, these sacraments welcome us into the Church.

What do I know about my Baptism?

Did You Know?

The baptized person always wears a white garment.

Baptism gives us new life in Christ.

The **Sacrament of Baptism** is the first of the Seven Sacraments. It gives us new life in Christ through the Holy Spirit. Baptism unites us with Jesus. It is the beginning of our new life with Jesus in his Church. All people who have been baptized are part of the Body of Christ.

Faith Word

Baptism the first sacrament we receive, which gives us new life in Jesus

"See what love the Father has bestowed on us that we may be called the children of God."

1 John 3:1

We receive the Sacrament of Baptism only once. Some people are baptized when they are infants. Others are baptized when they are older.

When we are baptized, we are welcomed into the Church. During Baptism, we are placed in water three times, or water is poured on us three times. The priest calls us by our name and then says: "I baptize you in the name of the Father, and of the Son, and of the Holy Spirit" (*Rite of Baptism,* 60). Each one of us was baptized with water and these same words.

Faith Word

grace God's life in us

At Baptism, we receive **grace**. Grace is a gift from God. It is his life in us. Grace makes us holy. It helps us grow as God's children.

Activity

Babies are often baptized at a font. This is a special container filled with holy water. Draw the symbols of Baptism on the font.

The **water** reminds us of new life in Christ.
A **shell** holds the water that is poured on us.
The **cross** reminds us of Jesus.

The next time you go to Mass, see if you can find the baptismal font.

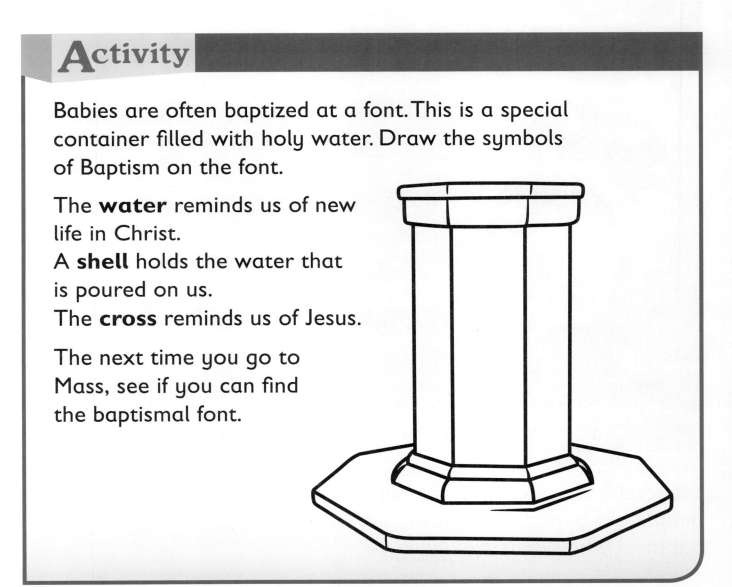

Confirmation strengthens our life in Christ.

In the **Sacrament of Confirmation**, God gives us help to live our Baptism. Confirmation is the sacrament that makes us stronger with the Gift of the Holy Spirit. We first receive the Holy Spirit when we are baptized. At Confirmation, the Holy Spirit gives us more strength to follow Jesus. This helps us to live our faith even when it is hard to do so.

Many people are confirmed when they are older children or young adults. People are confirmed only once. Confirmation lasts forever, just like Baptism.

A bishop is usually the person who confirms people. He lays his hands on each person and prays. The bishop dips his thumb in holy oil. He traces a cross on each person's forehead and says: "Be sealed with the Gift of the Holy Spirit" (*The Order of Confirmation*, 27).

Faith Word

Confirmation
the sacrament that strengthens us with the Gift of the Holy Spirit

The Eucharist unites us to Jesus.

On the night before Jesus died, he shared a meal with his followers. We call this meal the **Last Supper**. Jesus shared the gift of his Body and Blood in the form of bread and wine. Jesus asked his followers to remember him.

Every time the Church celebrates Mass, bread and wine become the Body and Blood of Jesus Christ, just as they did at the Last Supper. This is done through the words and actions of the priest, by the power of the Holy Spirit. Only a priest can lead us in the celebration of Mass.

Jesus is really present with us in the Eucharist. The **Sacrament of the Eucharist** is the sacrament of the Body and Blood of Jesus Christ. The Eucharist brings us more fully into the Church. Most Catholics receive the Eucharist for the first time when they are children. The Eucharist is the Church's most important sacrament. It unites us with Christ and one another in a special way.

Faith Words

Last Supper the meal that Jesus shared with his followers on the night before he died

Eucharist the sacrament of the Body and Blood of Jesus Christ

Activity

Color in the heart to remind you of Jesus.

Faith Words

Baptism   grace   Confirmation

Last Supper   Eucharist

 Show What You Know

Circle the term that answers the question.

1. What is the first sacrament we receive?

Eucharist | Baptism

2. What is God's gift of his life in us?

Last Supper | grace

3. Which sacrament strengthens us with the Gift of the Holy Spirit?

Confirmation | Baptism

Partners in Faith

Saint Peter Claver

Saint Peter Claver helped many people. He gave them food. He gave them medicine. He taught them about God. He baptized more than 300,000 people.

 Learn more about the life of Saint Peter Claver.

Copyright © by William H. Sadlier, Inc. All rights reserved.

How am I growing closer to God?

Mini-Task

Baptism, Confirmation, and the Eucharist are sacraments. The sacraments bring us closer to God.

Look at the symbols for each sacrament.

Baptism

Confirmation

Eucharist

Using the symbols, make a card that shows others about each sacrament. Write a message of thanks to God for giving us the sacraments.

How are these sacraments the same? How are they different? Talk about your card with a partner.

 Want to do more? Go to your Portfolio to continue this activity.

Talk with your family about your Baptism. Where was it celebrated? Who was there to celebrate with you?

Copyright © by William H. Sadlier, Inc. All rights reserved.

God is always with us. He loves us and wants us to love others. Jesus showed us how much God loves us. He helped people. He healed people. He forgave people for their sins. Today, the Church celebrates the Sacraments of Healing. Jesus gave us these sacraments. He wants us to trust that God's love is more powerful than sin or sickness.

Go to the digital portal for a prayer of petition.

"May almighty God have mercy on us, forgive us our sins, and bring us to everlasting life."

Roman Missal

Jesus showed us God's love by the things he said and did.

Jesus shared many truths about God the Father. He said God is like a shepherd who looks for the sheep that wandered away. God is like a father who welcomes back a child who ran away. These truths help us know that God loves us and wants us to be with him.

The most important thing Jesus taught us is to love God above all else and love our neighbor as ourselves.

Jesus always acted with love. We live the way God wants us to live when we love others as Jesus did.

What loving things do I do for others?

Did You Know?

Jesus' stories are shared throughout the world.

People asked Jesus for help.

Jesus loved everyone. He taught people about God's great love for us. He welcomed and blessed children. He comforted people who were sad or afraid. Jesus helped those who were poor. He fed those who were hungry. He healed people who were sick. News about Jesus spread everywhere. Crowds of people came to meet him.

"You shall love the Lord, your God, with all your heart, with all your soul, and with all your mind. This is the greatest and the first commandment. The second is like it: You shall love your neighbor as yourself."

Matthew 22:37–39

We need Jesus to help us, too. When we are sick or sad, Jesus wants us to turn to him. When we do not follow God's laws, Jesus wants us to say we are sorry. Jesus is always ready to help us!

Activity

Jesus wants us to ask him for help. What is something a first-grader might ask for? Write your answer here. Share with your class or group.

_____

_____

Jesus showed God's love by forgiving people.

Sometimes we do not love in the way that Jesus taught. **Sin** is any thought, word, or action that we do on purpose even though we know that it is wrong.

Jesus taught that God always loves us. When we sin, God wants us to ask for his forgiveness through the Church. God will always forgive us if we turn back to him. He forgives us when we are truly sorry and when we try to do better.

God wants us to forgive others, too. *To forgive* means "to accept someone's sorrow for doing something wrong." It is not always easy to forgive. God wants us to show love.

Faith Word

sin any thought, word, or action that we do on purpose even though we know that it is wrong

Activity

When we do something wrong, we can ask God for forgiveness. We say we are sorry. Pray this prayer.

> Dear Jesus,
> I'm sorry I sinned.
> Please forgive me.
> Help me to forgive others, too.
> Amen.

Practice the prayer to learn it by heart.

The **Sacrament of Penance and Reconciliation** is the sacrament in which we receive and celebrate God's forgiveness. We need God's forgiveness to live as his friends again.

In the Sacrament of Penance and Reconciliation, we talk with a priest about the ways we know we have sinned. We tell God we are sorry for what we have done wrong. We promise to try to avoid those sins in the future. Then the priest shares God's forgiveness with us.

We can celebrate the sacrament any time we need to be forgiven.

Faith Word

Penance and Reconciliation the sacrament in which we receive and celebrate God's forgiveness

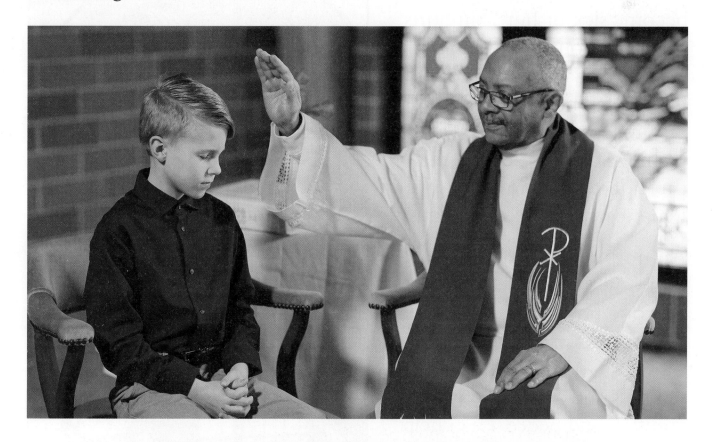

 "With you is forgiveness."

Psalm 130:4

Jesus showed God's love by healing people.

Jesus shows how much God the Father cares for us in the **Sacrament of the Anointing of the Sick**. Today, the Church celebrates this sacrament for people who are sick or hurting and in need of healing. In the sacrament, the priest prays for the Holy Spirit to bring comfort and peace to those who are sick.

Faith Word

Anointing of the Sick the sacrament in which the priest prays for the Holy Spirit to bring God's comfort and peace to those who are sick

We are all in need of healing. Sometimes our bodies can become sick or hurt. Sin hurts us. It hurts our friendship with God. When we sin, we cannot fix our friendship with God by ourselves. God must offer us his healing. He does this through the Sacrament of Penance and Reconciliation.

Anointing of the Sick along with Penance and Reconciliation are both Sacraments of Healing. They show us God's power over sickness and sin. They bring us comfort and peace. They help us live in friendship with God.

Faith Words

Penance and Reconciliation
Anointing of the Sick   sin

 Show What You Know

Circle the correct term to complete the sentence.

1. _____ is the sacrament in which the priest prays for the Holy Spirit to bring God's comfort and peace to those who are sick.

   Anointing of the Sick | Penance and Reconciliation

2. A _____ is any thought, word, or action that we do on purpose even though we know that it is wrong.

   sign | sin

Partners in Faith

Saint Peregrine Laziosi

Saint Peregrine Laziosi was very sick. He prayed to Jesus. He put all his faith in God. Saint Peregrine is an example of faith for all people who are sick and need comfort.

 Learn more about the life of Saint Peregrine Laziosi.

Copyright © by William H. Sadlier, Inc. All rights reserved.

How do I ask Jesus for help and healing?

Mini-Task

Jesus is always ready to help us. We can ask Jesus for help for ourselves.

Write a prayer to Jesus to help you.

_____

_____

We can ask Jesus to help others.

Write a prayer to Jesus to help a person who needs help or healing.

_____

_____

 Want to do more? Go to your Portfolio to continue this activity.

 **At Home**

Jesus is always with us to help us forgive and love more. Together, thank Jesus for being with your family.

Copyright © by William H. Sadlier, Inc. All rights reserved.

Jesus told us to love and serve God with our whole heart. We do this by loving and serving one another. God calls some women and men to marry. He calls some men to be priests. We all have a role to play. One way in which we love and serve others is by sharing God's love at home.

Go to the digital portal for a prayer of praise.

"The Church is nothing other than the family of God."

Catechism of the Catholic Church, 1655

Everyone plays a part in God's Church.

Jesus makes the Church holy. Because we are members of the Church, Jesus gives us the strength to be holy. Every member of the Church shows God's love by serving God and others. Some people teach us about Jesus. Some people lead us in prayer. Some people care for those who are sick or in need. Whatever they do, all baptized people play a part in the Church.

The work of the Church is the work of Jesus Christ. We are the Body of Christ. The work of the Church is our work, too! We have a role to play. We worship God together at Mass. We pray for one another. We help one another.

What gift do I use to serve God and others?

Did You Know?

 Everyone has gifts to share with others.

God calls us to service.

God wants all of us to share our gifts with others. When we serve, we use our gifts out of love to help others. Jesus taught his followers how to serve others. You can show kindness to someone who is sad. You can share the things that are yours. You can be a friend to someone who needs one. You can help keep your home and neighborhood clean.

When you serve others, you also serve God and the Church. Jesus wants us to use our gifts for the Church and for one another.

"As the Father has sent me, so I send you."
John 20:21

Activity

God has a role for each of us. Write the names of people you know on the lines.

_____ and _____ are married.
They serve God together in their family.
_____ is a priest.
He serves God in the parish community.
Right now, I will serve others by

_____ .

God asks some men to lead the Church as priests or deacons. He asks some men and women to serve together in a marriage as husband and wife. God has a role for each one of us!

The **Sacrament of Holy Orders** is a Sacrament at the Service of Communion. In the Sacrament of Holy Orders, a baptized man becomes a bishop, a priest, or a deacon. These men promise to spend their lives sharing God's love with people. Bishops, priests, and deacons share the message of Jesus. They teach us about our faith. They help us to live as Jesus did.

Faith Words

Holy Orders the sacrament in which a baptized man becomes a deacon, a priest, or a bishop

Matrimony the sacrament in which a baptized man and baptized woman become husband and wife

The **Sacrament of Matrimony** is also a Sacrament at the Service of Communion. Through Matrimony, a baptized man and a baptized woman become husband and wife. They promise to love and be faithful to each other always. Married people share God's love in special ways with each other and with their children. Married people love each other as Christ loves his Church.

We learn about Jesus in our families.

Married people teach their children about Jesus and the Church. They show their children how to live as followers of Jesus. The first place we learn about Jesus is in our family. We usually first learn to pray with our family.

Faith Word

Holy Family the family of Jesus, Mary, and Joseph

One of the most important ways for a family to learn about Jesus is by going to Mass together on Sunday. Families can show their love for God and one another in other ways, too. They can pray before meals or before bed. They can read stories from the Bible together. They can celebrate the seasons of the Church year at home.

Jesus grew up in a family, too. Jesus, Mary, and Joseph lived together in their home in Nazareth. They loved and cared for one another. Jesus obeyed Mary and Joseph. We call Jesus, Mary, and Joseph the **Holy Family**.

We share God's love in our families.

The first members of the Church were like a close family. They ate their meals together. They shared what they had. They praised God together.

Our families love and share with one another, too. Someone in your family makes sure you have food to eat and clothes to wear. Someone in your family might help you do your best in school. Someone takes care of you when you are sick.

God wants us to share his love in our families. A family shares God's love when they are kind and helpful. A family shares God's love when they do what Jesus asks us to do. A family shares God's love when they say they are sorry and forgive one another.

> "As I have loved you, so you also should love one another."
>
> John 13:34

Activity

One way we share God's love is by helping at home. Look at the chart. Put a check mark next to the ways you help. Circle one new thing to do this week.

- ☐ make my bed
- ☐ pick up my toys
- ☐ sort recycling
- ☐ clear the table
- ☐ say grace before dinner
- ☐ say bedtime prayers

Faith Words

Holy Orders   Matrimony

Holy Family

 Show What You Know

Match the terms to the correct definitions.

1. Holy Family

2. Matrimony

3. Holy Orders

the sacrament in which a baptized man becomes a bishop, a priest, or a deacon

Jesus, Mary, and Joseph

the sacrament in which a baptized man and baptized woman become husband and wife

Partners in Faith
Saint Zita

Saint Zita loved God and shared her love with others. She lived every day as a prayer to God. Saint Zita taught people that whatever we do, we can do it in praise of Jesus.

 Learn more about the life of Saint Zita.

Copyright © by William H. Sadlier, Inc. All rights reserved.

Mini-Task

God calls everyone to service. First-graders serve God in many ways. Here are some ways:

- Pray to God each morning and night.

- Be kind to other children at school.

- Do chores at home to help your family.

- Offer to visit an elderly relative or neighbor.

Write a way you can serve God today.

_____

_____

_____

Talk to a partner about ways to serve God and others.

 Want to do more? Go to your Portfolio to continue this activity.

 At Home

We share God's love every day in our families. In your family, tell one another how each person's kindness helps you know God's love.

Copyright © by William H. Sadlier, Inc. All rights reserved.

How do we live what we believe?

לא תרצח
לא תנאף
לא תגנב
תענה
לא תחמד את

The Ten Commandments

Unit Prayer

Leader: Saint Francis of Assisi taught us a prayer that is well known throughout the world. The prayer is all about living the way Jesus taught us. Saint Francis prayed: "Lord, make me an instrument of your peace."

Let us listen to how we can become people of peace.

Lord, where there is hatred, let me bring love.

All: Lord, make me an instrument of your peace.

Leader: Lord, when someone is hurting, make me an instrument of your peace.

All: Lord, make me an instrument of your peace.

Leader: When someone is afraid or alone, make me an instrument of your peace.

All: Lord, make me an instrument of your peace.

Leader: When someone is sad, let me bring him or her joy.

All: Lord, make me an instrument of your peace.

All sing: "Prayer of St. Francis"

Unit Song: "Prayer of St. Francis," Sebastian Temple/OCP

Missionary Discipleship

Do you remember a time when you were sad and someone made you feel better? Or maybe even laugh? How did you feel? When have you made someone who was sad or afraid feel better?

How do we know God loves us?

God loves and cares for all people. He wants us to love and care for one another, too. God gives us laws to help us. God's laws help us to know what he wants us to do. They help us to make good choices. Following God's laws leads us to love others and live as God's children.

 Go to the digital portal for a prayer of thanksgiving.

"Trust in the LORD and do good."

Psalm 37:3

We are made in the image and likeness of God.

God shared his love by creating human beings.
God made us to be like him.

- We can think and learn.

- We can care for the world.

- We can share love with our families and friends.

- We can listen to God and talk to him.

Every person God made is holy. We are holy because God is holy. We are holy because God made us to be like him. Everything good about us is because of God's goodness.

God made us to share in his love. God made us so that we could know him and love him. God made us to live in happiness with him forever.

In what ways do I show God's goodness?

Did You Know?

 Children care for God's world in many ways.

God loves everyone.

Jesus taught us that God is Father to us all. He loves each one of us equally. God made us all to be like him, but no two people are the same. We are all different from one another, just as God made us to be!

 "I praise you, because I am wonderfully made."
Psalm 139:14

Every person is different, and every person is special to God. God wants us to treat one another with kindness and respect. God wants us to treat one another like the holy people he made us to be.

God wants us to love him and to love one another as he loves us. He made us to take care of one another.

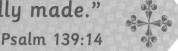

God helps us make good choices.

God wants us to love him and others. God never forces us to do this. He lets us choose for ourselves.

We make choices every day. Jesus made choices, too. He chose to love everyone. God lets us choose to act like Jesus or not. We can choose to share with others. We can help people in need. We can be kind and fair. When we choose to act like Jesus, we help share God's love with others. We live as God made us to live.

Activity

Work with a partner to write two good choices or actions and two bad choices or actions.

Good choices or actions:

_____

_____

Bad choices or actions:

_____

_____

Talk with another pair of partners about why the choices and actions are good or bad.

When we choose to do hurtful things, we are saying "no" to God. We are not living as God made us to live.

Faith Word

commandments laws that God gave us

God gave us laws to help us know how he wants us to live. God's laws are called **commandments**. When we follow God's commandments, they help us choose what God wants.

It is not always easy to choose what is right for us and for others. Jesus sent the Holy Spirit to help us make the right choices. We can ask the Holy Spirit to help us do what is right!

God's laws lead us to love others.

Jesus gave us the **Great Commandment.** The Great Commandment is Jesus' teaching to love God above all else and our neighbor as ourselves.

Jesus showed us how to follow the Great Commandment by everything he said and did. Jesus fed hungry people. He helped people even when he felt tired. He welcomed children when they ran up to meet him. Jesus did these things even when others did not agree with him.

Jesus wants us to follow his example. He taught us to love and care for all of God's children. Following God's commandments helps us to do this.

God's laws show us how to be good. They help us treat one another with love. When we obey the Great Commandment, it leads us to follow all of God's laws. The Great Commandment helps us love others as Jesus taught.

Activity

Describe one way you love God, yourself, or others.

_____

_____

Talk with a friend about the ways you love God or others.

Faith Words

commandments
Great Commandment

 Show What You Know

Circle the correct answer.

1. God's rules are called _____ .

   commitments | commandments

2. The _____ Commandment is Jesus' teaching to love God above all and our neighbor as ourselves.

   Great | First

Partners in Faith

Saint Thomas of Villanova

Saint Thomas of Villanova was a Spanish monk and teacher. He tried to live the Great Commandment in everything he did. Saint Thomas helped people find work. He also took care of children. Some people called Saint Thomas the "father of the poor."

 Learn more about the life of Saint Thomas of Villanova.

Copyright © by William H. Sadlier, Inc. All rights reserved.

How do God's laws help us to love?

Mini-Task

God gave us laws to show us how to live. God's laws show us how to be good. They help us treat one another with love and respect.

What do you do to treat others with kindness and respect? Write or draw one way that you follow God's law.

Turn and talk to a partner.

How does this law help keep you or others happy and safe?

 Want to do more? Go to your Portfolio to continue this activity.

At Home

Have each member of your family share God's love with another family member. He or she might help that person with a chore, listen carefully, or play a game.

Copyright © by William H. Sadlier, Inc. All rights reserved.

How do we respond to God's love?

God wants us to do good. He helps us to know right from wrong. Listening to our hearts helps us make good choices. God also gives us graces to help us live in friendship with him and one another. The good things we do are virtues. Faith, hope, and love are virtues that come from God. They help us treat everyone as part of God's family.

Go to the digital portal for a prayer of petition.

Do "what is good."
Gaudium et Spes, 17

God's plan is for us to be happy.

God created us to be happy with him forever in heaven. In heaven, we will feel no pain or sadness. We will have all that we need.

Jesus taught that we can be happy forever in heaven if we live as his followers now.

Faith Word

Beatitudes teachings of Jesus that describe the way to live as his followers

To help us with this, Jesus gave us the **Beatitudes**. The Beatitudes teach us how to be kind and treat others fairly at all times.

If we follow the Beatitudes, we will live in love as Jesus did. We will be true followers of Jesus.

> "Rejoice and be glad, for your reward will be great in heaven."
>
> Matthew 5:12

What makes me happy?

Did You Know?

Being happy is good for you.

God wants us to do good and listen to our hearts.

God wants us to think about the things we say and do. He asks us to choose to love him and others. He sent his Son, Jesus, to show us how to live. When we do as Jesus taught, we live as God wants us to.

This is not always easy. Sometimes we are not sure what is right and what is wrong. Sometimes we have to be quiet and listen to our hearts. God speaks in our hearts to help us to know what is right. God helps us make good choices.

Activity

God wants us to be happy and to do what is good. Draw a picture of a good choice, or write about one, that you can make this week.

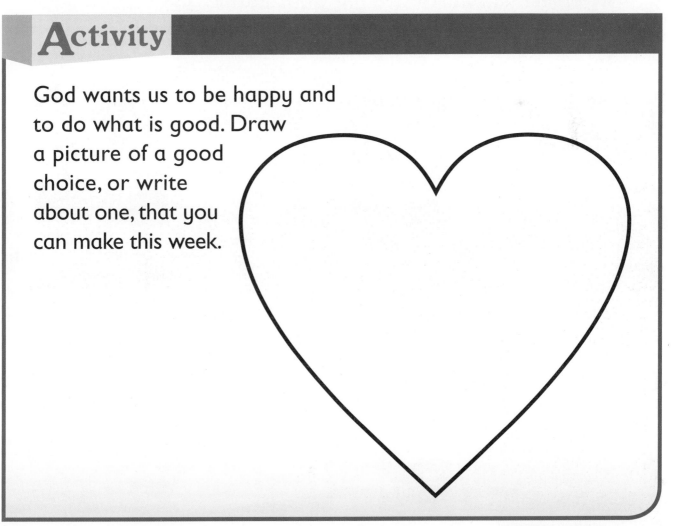

How do you know when your heart tells you that something is wrong? Maybe a parent or teacher reminds you. Or you might feel sad about making a wrong choice. You might feel worried. You know you want to do the right thing.

God wants us to listen to our hearts. He also wants us to learn about his laws. We learn about God's laws in the Bible. We also learn about God's laws from the Church. When we learn about God's laws and listen to our hearts, we can make the loving choices God wants for us.

 "Trust in the LORD with all your heart, . . . he will make straight your paths."

Proverbs 3:5–6

Virtues help us live in friendship with God.

God helps us to choose what is good. **Virtues** are good habits. Virtues help us act as God wants us to. Some virtues we develop through practice. Patience is an example of these virtues. Other virtues come from God. Faith, hope, and love are virtues that come from God. They help us live in friendship with God and with one another. Faith, hope, and love guide us as we choose right from wrong. The more we choose them, the stronger they grow.

Faith Word

virtue a good habit that helps us act as God wants us to

The Holy Spirit also guides us to make good choices. The Holy Spirit filled the Apostles with courage. The Holy Spirit made the Apostles strong followers of Jesus. The Holy Spirit helps us in the same way. The Holy Spirit helps us do what Jesus taught, even when doing that is hard.

Activity

The symbol for love is a heart. Tell a friend why you think a heart is a good symbol for the virtue of love.

We live in peace when we show love for others.

Faith Word

just fair

Jesus wanted his followers to get along and take care of one another. God made us to be one family, just as the Blessed Trinity is one. Jesus said: "I pray . . . that they may all be one, as you, Father, are in me and I in you, that they also may be in us" (John 17:20–21).

God wants us to work together to make sure our world is **just**. *Just* is a word that means "fair." We are fair when we are kind and truthful. We are just when we treat people equally. We are just when we try to make sure all people have what they need.

God wants us to live in peace and to love others. We do this when we show respect, when we play fair, and when we help those in need. We must work together to make sure every person can live the life God wants for him or her.

Faith Words

virtue　　　just　　　Beatitudes

 Show What You Know

Put a check mark next to the correct answer.

1. Jesus gave us _____ to help us live as his followers.
   - ☐ Beatitudes　　　☐ directions

2. A virtue is a _____ habit that helps us act as God wants us to.
   - ☐ bad　　　☐ good

3. God wants us to work together to make sure our world is

   _____ .
   - ☐ just　　　☐ busy

Write the answer to the question.

Where do the virtues of faith, hope, and love come

from? _____

Partners in Faith

Saint Philip Neri

Saint Philip loved to laugh. He loved to tell jokes. He knew that God's plan for us is to be happy with God forever.

 Learn more about the life of Saint Philip Neri.

Copyright © by William H. Sadlier, Inc. All rights reserved.

WITNESS 117

How can I do what is just?

Mini-Task

God wants us to work together to make sure our world is just. *Just* is a word that means "fair."

Write a story about one way you can be fair with someone else. Use the storyboard below.

Share your story with the group.

 Want to do more? Go to your Portfolio to continue this activity.

At Home

Have each person in your family choose one of the virtues of faith, hope, and love. Ask each person to share how he or she can live out that virtue.

Copyright © by William H. Sadlier, Inc. All rights reserved.

God gave us commandments because he loves us. God's commandments teach us how to love him above all else and our neighbor as ourselves. Our Church leaders help us to understand God's laws. They help us to follow God's laws. The Holy Spirit guides our Church leaders. We show that we believe in God and love him above all things when we obey his commandments.

Go to the digital portal for a *Lectio* and *Visio Divina* prayer.

"LORD, show me your way."

Psalm 27:11

God's laws help us love him and others.

Many years before Jesus was born, God gave his people special laws. These laws are called the **Ten Commandments**. They are written in the Bible. When Jesus was growing up, he knew these laws. He obeyed the commandments. Jesus taught his followers to obey them, too. Through his example, he showed people what it means to follow them. Jesus said: "If you love me, you will keep my commandments" (John 14:15).

Faith Word

Ten Commandments
ten special laws God gave to his people

God gave us the Ten Commandments because he loves us and wants us to be happy. Not following the commandments hurts us. It may also hurt other people. It hurts our friendship with God.

We show our love for God above all else by obeying the Ten Commandments. We also show love for our neighbor as ourselves. The commandments help us to live as God's children.

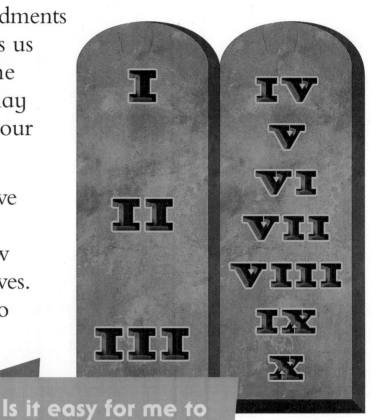

Is it easy for me to follow rules?

Did You Know?

 There are laws all around us.

Sunday is the Lord's Day.

God gives us laws because he loves us. We show our love for God when we obey his commandments.

The first three of the Ten Commandments help us to love God.

1. Believe in One God.

2. Speak God's name with respect.

3. Honor the Lord's Day.

The Church calls Sunday the Lord's Day. On Sunday, we celebrate that Jesus rose from the dead on the first day of the week. We remember this each week by going to Mass.

The Church also gives us laws that help us follow God's laws. One of the laws of the Church is that we should attend Mass on Sundays. This helps us make the Lord's Day holy, as the Ten Commandments tell us to do.

There are many ways to honor the Lord's Day. We go to Mass with our families on Saturday evening or on Sunday. We do not do work that can wait for another time. We show love to our families and others. Sunday is a day to praise and thank God for his many gifts.

Activity

Draw one way that you can make Sunday special. Share your drawing with the group.

We show our love for God by the way we love others.

The first three of the Ten Commandments help us to love God. The other seven of the Ten Commandments help us to love our neighbor as ourselves.

How do we follow these commandments?

4. We obey our parents and all who take their place.

5. We respect all human life.

6. We respect our bodies and the bodies of others.

7. We do not take anything that is not ours.

8. We tell the truth.

9. We are thankful for our own family and friends.

10. We are thankful for what we own and do not get jealous of what others own.

God wants us to show our love for him by the way we treat the people he created. Jesus said: "I give you a new commandment: love one another. As I have loved you, so you also should love one another" (John 13:34).

When we love others as Jesus did, we show that we are followers of Jesus. We love one another by following the Ten Commandments. When we obey these commandments, we show that we love God by being good to others.

Activity

The Fourth Commandment tells us to obey our parents. What is one way you obey your parents? Tell a friend about it.

The Holy Spirit helps our Church leaders.

The Church helps us follow the Ten Commandments and live as God's children. The Holy Spirit guides our Church leaders.

When we are strong and faithful, we help the whole Church to be strong and faithful. Our Church leaders help us to be strong members of the Body of Christ. They remind us of God's laws and help us know how to follow them. They remind us to go to Mass on Sundays and other holy days. They encourage us to receive the sacraments regularly.

Obeying the laws of the Church helps us to follow Jesus.

Faith Word

Ten Commandments

 Show What You Know

Circle the correct answer.

1. The first _____ of the commandments help us love God.

   two | three

2. Sunday is the _____ Day.

   Lord's | Last

3. The Church helps us know God's _____ and follow them.

   laws | paths

Write the answer to the question.

How many commandments did God give us?

_____

Partners in Faith

Saint Gregory of Nazianzen

Saint Gregory was a bishop. He wanted to be a priest. He followed God's will. He helped teach the truth about Jesus.

 Learn more about the life of Saint Gregory of Nazianzen.

Copyright © by William H. Sadlier, Inc. All rights reserved.

How do I love God and others?

Mini-Task

The Ten Commandments help us to love God and others.

Make a poster about the commandments.

 Want to do more? Go to your Portfolio to continue this activity.

At Home

Talk about your family's rules. How do they help people in your family show love?

Copyright © by William H. Sadlier, Inc. All rights reserved.

What turns us away from God's love?

God loves us. He wants us to love him and follow his laws. Sometimes we turn away from God's love. We do things we know are wrong. We do not love as Jesus taught us. Sin is a choice to disobey God. There are different kinds of sins, but they all hurt our friendship with God and others. Yet God always loves us. He forgives us when we are sorry and promise not to sin again.

Go to the digital portal for a prayer of petition.

"A clean heart create for me, God."

Psalm 51:12

Original Sin separates us from God.

God made the first man and woman. He let them share in his own life, but they sinned. They disobeyed God. That first sin is called **Original Sin**.

Original Sin was passed down to all people. We are born with Original Sin. Baptism takes away Original Sin and all other personal sins. When we were baptized, we were freed from sin and given a share in God's life.

Human beings are not perfect like God. Sometimes we choose to do things that we know are wrong. Sin hurts us. It hurts our friendship with God. Sin separates us from God and others.

Faith Word

Original Sin the first sin, committed when the first man and woman, Adam and Eve, disobeyed God

What are some ways that sin hurts?

Did You Know?

 No one is perfect.

Sin is a choice to disobey God.

Sin is any thought, word, or action that we choose to do even though we know that it is not what God wants. When we commit a sin, we disobey God.

We cannot commit a sin by accident. Sometimes we make bad choices by mistake. Sometimes we do not know that something is wrong. Sins are not mistakes or accidents. We sin when we choose to not follow God's laws. We sin when we choose something bad for ourselves or for others.

When we sin, we fail to love God, ourselves, or others as Jesus taught. When we sin, we are not living as God wants. Sin turns us away from God's love.

God wants us to love and obey him, but he never forces us to do this. God lets us choose. Every day, we make choices about what we do, think, and say. God lets us choose whether we will follow his commandments. He lets us choose whether we will love as Jesus taught.

Activity

A mistake or an accident is not a sin. Put a check mark next to the things that are sins. Put an X next to the things that are not sins.

Talk with a friend about how to tell what is a sin and what is not a sin.

Action	Sin	Not a Sin
Breaking a toy while playing	☐	☐
Telling a lie	☐	☐
Forgetting a chore	☐	☐

There are different kinds of sins.

All sins do harm. Some sins are so serious that they turn us away from God completely. People who commit these sins break their friendship with God. They do not share in God's grace.

Other sins are less serious. People who commit these sins hurt their friendship with God, but they still share in God's grace.

When we practice virtue, we become happier and more loving. When we choose small sins again and again, we may become selfish and unloving. We may become lazy about doing what God wants. Even small sins can become serious if we commit them over and over. We may hurt others often.

The Holy Spirit can help us build loving habits instead. By getting into the habit of doing good, we sin less often. We obey God's laws and live as he wants us to.

We hurt ourselves and others when we choose to sin.

God made us to live as one family, just as the Blessed Trinity is One. He wants all people to live in unity. Living in unity means we live together as one group of people. When one person sins, it hurts all of us.

The Church is made strong and holy through Christ. She is also made strong and holy through his love that we show to others. When we sin, we hurt our human family and the Church. The Bible says: "If [one] part suffers, all the parts suffer with it" (1 Corinthians 12:26).

Even when we sin, God still loves us. When we tell God we are sorry and promise to do our best not to sin again, God will always forgive us.

Activity

Write the word *love* on a clean sheet of paper. Crumple the paper into a ball. Pass your paper to a friend. Ask your friend if he or she can see what you wrote.

Talk with a friend about how sin hides the love in our hearts, just as the crumpled paper makes it hard to see the word *love*.

Faith Word

Original Sin

 Show What You Know

Circle the correct answer.

1. The first sin is called _____ .

Original Sin | Only Sin

2. God made us all to live as one _____ .

friendship | family

3. All sins do _____ .

harm | help

Write the answer to the question.

Are mistakes and accidents sins?

_____

Partners in Faith

Saint Dismas

God will always forgive us if we ask. Saint Dismas was with Jesus when Jesus died on the Cross. He asked Jesus for forgiveness. Jesus forgave Dismas.

 Learn more about the life of Saint Dismas.

Copyright © by William H. Sadlier, Inc. All rights reserved.

How do we show God's love?

Mini-Task

When we love God, ourselves, and others, we live in God's love as one family.

Look at the blocks. On each block, write an action that a first-grader could do to love God, self, or others.

Now pair and share. What did your friend write on his or her blocks?

Pair and share with a different friend. What did this friend write?

Imagine all the blocks coming together to build a structure.

How are the loving actions like blocks that make a building strong?

How do your good actions make the family of all God's people strong?

 Want to do more? Go to your Portfolio to continue this activity.

At Home

Sin hurts our family. Talk together about ways we can apologize to one another.

Copyright © by William H. Sadlier, Inc. All rights reserved.

What turns us toward God's love?

God wants us to turn away from sin and live in his friendship forever. God gives us the gift of grace to help us. Grace heals us from sin. It helps us choose what is loving and good. Through God's grace, we are forgiven for our sins and are able to live in God's love.

Go to the digital portal for a prayer of praise.

> "May almighty God have mercy on us,
> forgive us our sins,
> and bring us to everlasting life."
> Penitential Act, *Roman Missal*

God gives us gifts to make us strong.

Saint Peter was one of the Apostles that Jesus chose to follow him. Peter learned about God's love from Jesus. Even so, Peter did not always do what Jesus wanted. When Jesus was taken away to die, Peter was afraid for his own life. He turned away from Jesus. He said he did not even know Jesus.

Peter sinned by turning away from Jesus. With God's grace, Peter was sorry and asked for forgiveness.

God invites all of us to love and follow him. God invites us, just as Jesus invited Peter. God gives us many gifts to help us. God gives us our families, and the Church helps make us strong and holy.

How do I make up for my wrong choices?

Did You Know?

To offer a gift is to show love.

God also gives us his grace. God's grace is a gift. It helps us live as Jesus taught. God's grace helps us live as his children. Grace also helps us to turn back to God when we sin.

> "No one can come to me unless the Father who sent me draw him."
>
> John 6:44

In the end, God's grace helped Peter do what Jesus wanted. God's grace is a gift that helps us to follow Jesus and do what God wants.

Activity

God gives us gifts to help us do the right thing. Look at the top picture. What happened?

Now look at the other two pictures that show the choices the boy could make. Circle the choice you would make with God's grace to help you.

Share with a friend a time when God's grace helped you do the right thing.

God makes us his adopted daughters and sons.

There is only one Son of God: Jesus Christ. In Baptism, God makes us his adopted sons and daughters. We receive God's grace in Baptism. We come to share in God's own life. We become children of God and members of the Body of Christ.

God wants to share his love with us forever. He wants us to follow Jesus and obey his commandments. God gives us his grace to help us do this. It is because of God's grace that we can believe in Jesus. It is because of God's grace that we want to follow God and do his will.

Grace helps us live as God wants us to. It helps us love God above all else and our neighbor as ourselves. Grace helps us to live as children of God.

Grace heals us from sin.

God does not force us to do what is right. God always invites us. God gives us his grace to help us follow his commandments.

We all sin. Sometimes we do things that are selfish and unkind. We hurt ourselves and others. We hurt our friendship with God.

Grace helps our hearts to heal. Grace helps us to feel sorry for our sins and keep our promise not to sin again. With the grace of God and the power of the Holy Spirit, we can turn back to God. Grace heals us from sin and makes us holy. Grace helps us to love as Jesus taught and to live as God's children again.

Grace helps us to choose love instead of sin.

God loves us so much. God wants us to love him, too. He wants us to follow Jesus so that we can live with him forever in heaven.

When we sin, God is always ready to show us **mercy**. *Mercy* is another word for God's love and forgiveness. God gives us his grace to help us turn away from sin and turn back toward his love. God's grace helps us to ask for forgiveness when we sin.

God's grace also helps us forgive others. God wants us to show mercy to others. He wants us to forgive others just as he forgives us. Jesus said: "Be merciful, just as [also] your Father is merciful" (Luke 6:36).

Faith Word

mercy God's love and forgiveness

Activity

Act out how you could show mercy when someone blames you for something you did not do.

Trace the words to learn something you can say when you show mercy.

I forgive you.

Faith Word

mercy

 Show What You Know

Put an X on the wrong answer.

1. _____ helps our hearts to heal.

   Gratitude | Grace

2. God's love and forgiveness is called _____ .

   mercy | marriage

3. God wants to share his love with us _____ .

   sometimes | forever

Partners in Faith

Saint Philip the Apostle

Saint Philip was one of Jesus' Apostles. He told his friends about Jesus. He taught many people. He wanted everyone to love God.

 Learn more about the life of Saint Philip.

Copyright © by William H. Sadlier, Inc. All rights reserved.

How does God's grace help me?

Mini-Task

In this lesson, you learned about God's grace. Remember all of the ways that grace helps us.

Look back in your book. Then write in the web the ways God's grace helps us.

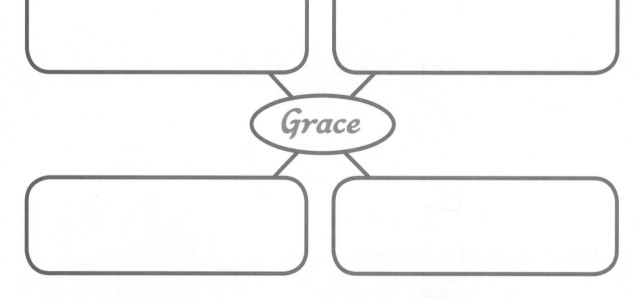

Grace

 Want to do more? Go to your Portfolio to continue this activity.

At Home

As a family, pray the Our Father. Pay special attention to the prayer's message of mercy and forgiveness.

Copyright © by William H. Sadlier, Inc. All rights reserved.

How do we become what we believe?

Jesus Praying on a Mountain

Unit Prayer

Leader: Saint Francis loved animals and all of God's creation. All of creation is a gift of love from God. Let us listen to how we can thank God for the gift of creation.

Let us pray: We thank you, O God, for our families. They help us to show our love for you and each other. Thank you for families.

All: Thank you for families.

Leader: We thank you, O God, for all animals. They make us happy and show us how much you love us. Thank you for animals.

All: Thank you for animals.

Leader: We thank you, O God, for flowers and trees, for rivers and oceans, for the sunshine and for rain. Thank you for nature.

All: Thank you for nature.

Leader: We thank you for Jesus, alive in our hearts.

All: Thank you for Jesus.

All sing: "We Are Marching"

 Unit Song: "We Are Marching," African/Traditional

Missionary Discipleship

How does God show us his love with flowers, trees, and all of nature? How have you shown your love for God by the way you take care of his creation?

What is prayer?

Prayer is talking and listening to God. We lift our hearts and minds to God in prayer. Most often, we pray to God the Father and to Jesus, his divine Son. God always hears us. God invites all people to pray to him in good times and in bad times. Prayer brings us closer to God.

 Go to the digital portal for a prayer of thanksgiving.

Prayer is the raising of one's mind and heart to God.

Saint John Damascene

We talk to God and listen to him in prayer.

Whom do you talk to when you are feeling sad? Whom do you talk to when you want to share happy news? Maybe you tell your family or a friend. Do you know you can also talk to God?

When we pray, we talk to God and listen to God. In our prayer, we can tell God when we are sad or worried. We can tell God when we feel happy or grateful. We can talk to God no matter how we feel. With God, we are never alone because he is always with us.

God wants us to talk to him in good times and in bad times. When we pray, we lift up our hearts and minds to God. We praise him; we thank him. We ask God for things we want or need. We also listen in our hearts to what God is saying.

To whom do I like to talk?

Did You Know?

 God speaks to us in prayer.

God calls his people in prayer.

The Bible tells about two sisters Jesus visited, named Martha and Mary. Martha worked to prepare food for Jesus.

"[Martha] had a sister named Mary [who] sat beside the Lord at his feet listening to him speak. Martha . . . came to [Jesus] and said, 'Lord, do you not care that my sister has left me by myself to do the serving? Tell her to help me.' The Lord said to her in reply, 'Martha, Martha, you are anxious and worried about many things. There is need of only one thing. Mary has chosen the better part and it will not be taken from her.'" (Luke 10:39–42)

Martha welcomed and served Jesus, but Mary listened to him. Mary opened her mind and heart to Jesus. This is what God invites us to do in prayer.

God calls each one of us to spend time talking with him and listening to him. When we pray, we open our minds and hearts to God as Mary did.

Activity

Draw a picture of something you talk to God about.

Share your drawing with the group. Tell how you feel when you talk to God.

We can always talk to God.

God **invites** all people to open their hearts and minds to him. Prayer is how humans have always talked to God and listened to him. God never stops calling each person to prayer.

Faith Word

invite to ask someone to do something

God made us. He knows us better than anyone. He knows what we are thinking, even when we keep our thoughts a secret from other people. God knows what is in our hearts.

You can always talk to God. He wants you to pray, no matter how you are feeling. God always loves us and listens to us.

Prayer is one way that we show we love God and want to be close to him.

Activity

God knows what is in our hearts. Write what is in your heart right now.

Share with a friend what you wrote. Ask about what is in your friend's heart.

God the Father hears our prayers.

Jesus prayed to his Father in heaven. Jesus taught us to call God "our Father," too, and to pray to him. When we pray to God the Father, we show that we trust in his love for us. We know that he hears our prayers.

God always answers our prayers. That does not mean God always gives us what we ask for. Sometimes when we ask for something, God says "no." Even when God says "no," he does so because he loves us.

When we pray, we show that we trust God to love and care for us, no matter what. We show that we want to be his children.

Faith Word

invite

 Show What You Know

Put a check mark next to the correct answer.

1. When we _____ , we talk with God and listen to him.
☐ play | ☐ pray

2. When we pray, we lift our _____ and minds to God.
☐ hearts | ☐ hands

3. _____ taught us to call God "our Father."
☐ Jesus | ☐ Martha

Write the answer to the question.

Who knows what is in our hearts?

_____

Partners in Faith

Saint Monica

Saint Monica wanted her son to live a better life. She prayed all the time. Finally, her son did the right thing. He became a follower of Jesus.

 Learn more about the life of Saint Monica.

Copyright © by William H. Sadlier, Inc. All rights reserved.

Mini-Task

God invites us to listen and talk to him.

When we talk with people, we need to try to understand what they are telling us. The same is true when we listen to God in prayer.

One way that many people prepare for prayer is with a prayer bowl. The prayer bowl can hold notes that remind us of what to say to God. They can also tell us ways to be ready to listen to God.

On the first two notes, write ideas for how to prepare for prayer. On the third note, write one thing you can talk to God about in prayer.

 Want to do more? Go to your Portfolio to continue this activity.

 At Home

We can talk to God at any time. Have members of your family tell God something they are happy about right now. As a family, say "Thank you" to God!

Copyright © by William H. Sadlier, Inc. All rights reserved.

Why do we pray?

Prayer keeps us close to God. We can pray wherever we are and whatever we are doing. The Church teaches us to pray together as God's children. Jesus is with us when we pray. He hears our prayers. Prayer helps us to become more like Jesus. When we pray often, it helps our love and trust in God grow strong.

Go to the digital portal for a meditation prayer.

"The LORD is near to all who call upon him."

Psalm 145:18

The Church teaches us to pray.

Jesus prayed to God, his Father. He taught his disciples to pray. Jesus promised to be with them when they prayed together. He said: "For where two or three are gathered together in my name, there am I in the midst of them" (Matthew 18:20).

The disciples gathered to **praise** God together. They prayed for one another and asked for God's help. The disciples passed on what Jesus taught. They helped new believers to pray.

The Church teaches us to pray. We pray with the Church as Jesus and his disciples taught. Jesus is with us when we pray. The Holy Spirit helps us. Prayer helps us to become more like Jesus.

What do I like about praying?

Did You Know?

Praying often with others is a good way to pray.

Prayer keeps us close to God.

God our Father made us because he loves us. He made us to be like him. When we pray, we show that we want to be holy, as God made us to be.

God the Father is always speaking in our hearts. He wants us to talk to him and to listen to him at all times. God wants all people to be close to him.

Prayer helps keep us close to God. When we pray, we remember that God is with us. We remember that God loves and cares for us. We remember that everything good comes from God. The more we pray, the more our love and trust in God grows.

Activity

Jesus is with us when we pray with others. Get into groups of two or three. Ask the other children in your group what they want to pray for. Remember that your prayer can start with:

• Thank you, God, for . . .

• God, please help . . .

• God, I am sorry for . . .

You can also use your own words. Pray together as a group.

We can pray anywhere.

It is good to have a special place where you can pray. This might be by your bed or in a corner of your room. You should also pray at church.

Jesus wants us to pray together with the Church the way the Apostles did. Jesus also wants us to pray wherever we are. We do not need to wait for just the right time or place to pray.

You can pray indoors and outdoors. You can pray alone and in a crowd. You can pray at church, home, or school. You can pray at any time of the day or night. God invites us to pray wherever we are, whatever we are doing.

No matter where we are, God is with us. He wants us to pray in good times and in bad times, when we are happy and when we are sad. God wants us to pray when things are busy and noisy and when things are calm and quiet. God always listens to our prayers, no matter what.

Activity

Think of three places where you like to pray. Write them here.

1. _____

2. _____

3. _____

Choose one of the places for a special prayer this week. Tell the group or a partner about the place you chose. Make a group list of places to pray.

God's children pray together.

It is good to pray with other people. The followers of Jesus prayed together often. Jesus wants us to pray together, too. There are many ways to do this.

- We can pray at home with our families.

- We can pray with our parish when we go to Mass on Sunday.

- We can join together for other special prayers of the Church.

- We can pray by reading the Bible together.

God tells us we are his children when we pray. By praying together often, we show that we love God and we want to be his children. Praying together is an important part of following Jesus.

Faith Word

praise

 Show What You Know

Circle the correct answer.

1. God the Father is always _____ in our hearts.

speaking | hiding

2. God _____ listens to our prayers.

always | sometimes

3. We can pray with our parish when we celebrate the _____ .

birthday | Mass

4. We _____ God because of his greatness.

praise | sing to

- -

Partners in Faith

Saint Brigid of Ireland

Saint Brigid took care of cows in a dairy. She prayed as she milked the cows and while she made butter. She prayed whenever she worked.

 Learn more about the life of Saint Brigid.

Copyright © by William H. Sadlier, Inc. All rights reserved.

Mini-Task

Make a Praise Spinner. Alone or with a partner, decide on three or four ways you can praise God. Your Praise Spinner can remind you to praise God every day. Or it can help you inspire a friend that we all need to praise God.

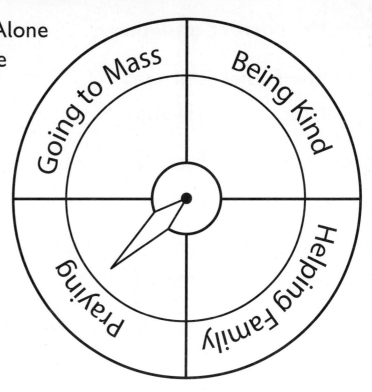

 Want to do more? Go to your Portfolio to continue this activity.

At Home

Ask your family members how you can pray for them, and let them know how to pray for you. Take a few moments together to pray tonight.

Copyright © by William H. Sadlier, Inc. All rights reserved.

How do we pray?

God wants us to pray every day. The Church also calls us to pray together at special times. The Holy Spirit helps us to pray in many ways. We praise God, bless him, and thank him. We ask God to help us or others. God always hears us, no matter how or when we pray.

Go to the digital portal for a prayer of praise.

"Call to me, and I will answer you." Jeremiah 33:3

We thank God for his many blessings.

God gives us many gifts. He gives us the world and our families. Most importantly, God gives us Jesus. We should say "Thank you" to God every day.

We pray to thank God. We praise and bless God. We ask God to help us and to forgive us for our sins. We pray for the needs of other people. No matter how, where, or when we pray, God is listening. God the Holy Spirit helps us in our prayers.

Who prays with me?

Did You Know?

 We can say "thank you" by the way we act.

Activity

Write one special thing you are thankful for.

_____

_____

Color a thank-you card for God.

Thank You!

We can pray at any time of the day.

God is always speaking to us. We can also talk to God in prayer anytime. Try saying these prayers silently to yourself during the day.

- In the morning: "God, thank you for this new day!"

- Before meals: "Father, please bless this food."

- When you need help: "Be with me, Lord."

- Before bed: "I am sorry for the ways I sinned today."

Our prayers do not need to be long. What matters is that we acknowledge God's presence and turn our hearts to him when we pray.

Sometimes our minds may wander when we pray. Sometimes our hearts may turn to other things. Prayer is a time to remember that God is with us. Whenever we pray, we should do our best to keep our attention on God.

Activity

Draw or write something you could pray about at different times of the day.

8 a.m.	Noon	8 p.m.

God always listens when we pray.

We should pray every day. We can pray alone and with our family. The Church also invites us to pray.

The Mass is the Church's most important prayer. At Mass, we thank God for his many gifts. We praise God and say we are sorry for our sins. We pray for our own needs, the needs of others, and the needs of the Church.

We use our bodies to help us pray at Mass. We stand to show respect to our Lord. We sit to show that we are listening and learning. We kneel to show honor and respect for Jesus Christ, who is with us in the Eucharist.

God hears all kinds of prayers.

We pray in many ways. We pray silently and out loud. We pray with the Bible and with holy objects. We even pray by sitting quietly and remembering that God is with us. God also invites us to pray from our hearts. God hears all our prayers, even when we do not say a word.

Faith Word

Lord's Prayer
the prayer
Jesus taught his
followers

Jesus prayed in all of these ways, too. Jesus also gave us a special prayer to God the Father. This prayer is called the **Lord's Prayer**. Sometimes we call it the Our Father. You will learn more about the Lord's Prayer later in your book.

The Church helps us to pray like Jesus. We pray the Glory Be to the Father prayer to the Blessed Trinity. In this prayer, we praise our One God in Three divine Persons. We remember that God always was and always will be.

We can say the Glory Be to the Father out loud or silently. We can pray it alone or with others.

Glory Be to the Father

Glory be to the Father
and to the Son
and to the Holy Spirit,
as it was in the beginning,
is now, and ever shall be
world without end.
Amen.

 Glory Be

Faith Word

Lord's Prayer

 Show What You Know

Circle the term that answers each question.

1. What prayer did Jesus teach his followers?

the Lord's Prayer | the Last Prayer

2. What prayer do we pray to the Blessed Trinity?

the Holy Be | the Glory Be to the Father

3. What is the Church's most important prayer?

the Mass | the Glory Be to the Father

Partners in Faith

Saint Charles Borromeo

Saint Charles Borromeo knew that we can talk to God wherever we are. He said that we can treat everything we do as a prayer.

 Learn more about the life of Saint Charles Borromeo.

Copyright © by William H. Sadlier, Inc. All rights reserved.

How do I thank God for his blessings?

Mini-Task

God's creation gives us the food we eat. Food makes our bodies strong and healthy. A lot of people work to bring God's gifts to our tables.

When we gather to eat, we can inspire others to be closer to God. Make a plan for a Gift-of-God table mat. List on your mat blessings you are thankful for. Then write ways you can show your thanks to God for those who prepared your meal.

Thank you, God, for the blessing of:

_____

Want to do more? Go to your Portfolio to continue this activity.

At Home

As a family, pray one of the prayers in this lesson. In the morning, say: "God, thank you for this new day." When you need help, pray: "Be with us, Lord." Allow each member of your family a turn to lead the prayer.

Copyright © by William H. Sadlier, Inc. All rights reserved.

What helps us to pray?

God gives us many gifts to help us pray. God gives us our families. God gives us the Church and the liturgy. God also gives us his own Word in the Bible. Even with all this help, it is sometimes hard to pray. God wants us to keep trying. Prayer opens our hearts to God and makes us holy.

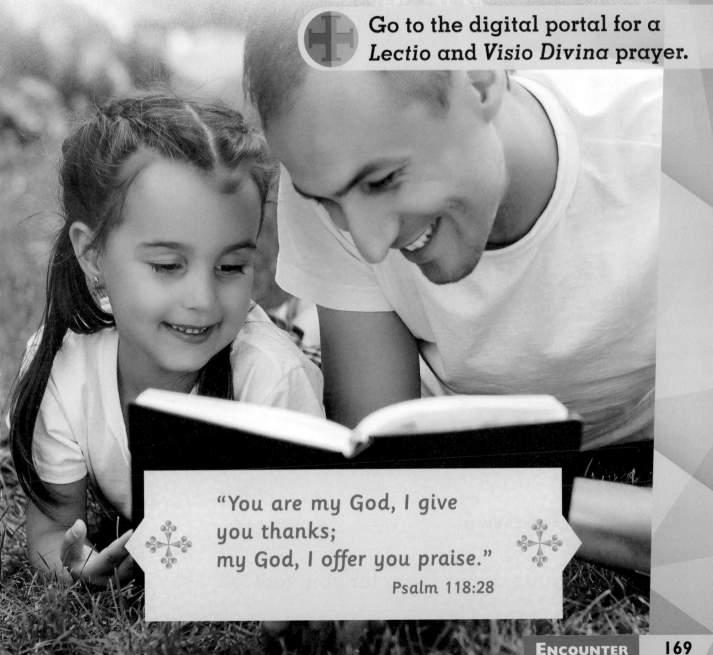

Go to the digital portal for a _Lectio_ and _Visio Divina_ prayer.

"You are my God, I give you thanks;
my God, I offer you praise."

Psalm 118:28

The Church is a family of believers.

God creates us to be his family. He gives us the Church to help us pray.

The Church is a family of believers. When we pray with the Church, we pray with those who are living and those who are in heaven. We pray for one another and for those who have died.

When we pray with the Church, we pray with the saints. We ask the saints to help us follow Jesus and live holy lives the way they did. We ask them to pray for us, just as we might ask a friend to pray for us.

Whom do I ask to pray for me?

Did You Know?

The saints are praying for you, too!

The Bible is God's Word for us.

The Bible also helps us to pray. The Bible is God's own Word to us. In the Bible, we learn about God the Father, the Son, and the Holy Spirit. We learn how Jesus prayed and taught his followers to pray.

Many prayers come from the Bible. The one you probably know best is the Lord's Prayer. Jesus taught this prayer to his followers. We pray the Lord's Prayer every time we celebrate Mass.

In the name of the Father,

and of the Son,

and of the Holy

Spirit.

Amen.

We use these same words every time we pray the Sign of the Cross. The priest also sends us into the world at the end of Mass, just as Jesus sent his disciples.

Listen carefully to the readings from the Bible at Mass. You can also pray with the Bible at home. You can read the words and stories in a children's Bible.

Read the Bible quietly to yourself, or ask your family to read it with you. Really try to pay attention to God's Word. God always has something special to tell us.

Activity

The words in the Hail Mary prayer come from the Bible. Ask someone to read aloud Luke 1:28–42 to you. What words are the same as the Hail Mary?

Hail Mary

Hail, Mary, full of grace, the Lord is with you!
Blessed are you among women,
and blessed is the fruit of your womb, Jesus.
Holy Mary, Mother of God,
pray for us sinners,
now and at the hour of our death.
Amen.

Pray the Hail Mary together as a group.

Families pray together.

The Church and the Bible help us to pray. Our families also help us to pray. God gives us our family to be our "Church at home." Praying with our family every day helps us grow closer to God.

Prayer brings families closer together. Prayer **unites** us. It helps our family to be one as the Blessed Trinity is One.

We should pray at home together and often. We can pray as we start our day, before meals, and at bedtime. We can ask God to keep our family safe and healthy. We can ask God to bless family members in need. Any time of the day is a good time to pray together.

Faith Word

unite to bring together

Prayer makes our hearts strong.

Even with all the help God gives us, it is not always easy to pray. We might feel bored or tired when we pray. We might think about other things, even when we do not mean to.

God wants us to keep trying when we find it hard to pray. We can ask the Holy Spirit to help us. Praying shows God that we want to live as his friends, even when it is hard. Praying makes our hearts grow strong and holy.

Prayer shows God that we love him. Try using this prayer to tell God you love him:

An Act of Love

O God, we love you above all things.
Help us to love our neighbor as ourselves
as Jesus taught us to do.

Activity

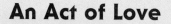

Memorize the Act of Love. Teach it to a friend. Then create a dance or other movement based on the prayer. Share your work with the group.

Faith Word

unite

 Show What You Know

Circle the correct term to complete the sentence.

1. We can ask the saints to _____ for us.

sing | pray

2. Prayer _____ us, or brings us together.

unites | uses

Partners in Faith

Saints Gregory and Nonna

Saint Gregory the Elder and Saint Nonna had two sons and a daughter who became saints. Their son Gregory the Younger became a famous writer in the Church.

 Learn more about the lives of Saints Gregory and Nonna.

Copyright © by William H. Sadlier, Inc. All rights reserved.

How do I pray for others and with others?

Mini-Task

Plan a Circle-of-Love prayer mobile with two separate circles. One circle says: "Whom do I pray with?" The other circle says: "Whom do I pray for?"

Whom do I pray with?

Whom do I pray for?

We can pray to God every day. God is always with us in every moment of our lives. From morning to night, we can pray to God in a circle of love.

Share your plan for the circles with the group.

 Want to do more? Go to your Portfolio to continue this activity.

At Home

Talk with your family about how praying together helps make your family a Church of the home and helps bring you closer to God. How can your family be a better Church?

Copyright © by William H. Sadlier, Inc. All rights reserved.

Why is the Lord's Prayer called the perfect prayer?

Jesus taught that God the Father is our Father, too. God the Father loves and cares for us. Jesus gave us the Lord's Prayer so that we could pray just like him, using his own words. The Lord's Prayer is special to the Church. When we pray the Lord's Prayer, we call God our Father, as Jesus taught us to do.

Go to the digital portal for a traditional prayer.

"Your Father knows what you need before you ask him."

Matthew 6:8

The Lord's Prayer is special to the Church.

Jesus taught that God, his Father, is our Father, too. He taught his followers how to pray to God the Father. We call the prayer that Jesus taught us the Lord's Prayer or the Our Father.

Lord's Prayer

Our Father, who art in heaven,
hallowed be thy name;
thy kingdom come;
thy will be done on earth as it is in heaven.
Give us this day our daily bread;
and forgive us our trespasses
as we forgive those who trespass against us;
and lead us not into temptation,
but deliver us from evil.
Amen.

The Lord's Prayer is special to the Church. It helps us love God and live as Jesus taught.

Who taught me how to pray?

Did You Know?

 God is our Father, too.

Jesus gave us this special prayer addressed to God the Father.

Jesus said: "The Father and I are one" (John 10:30). The Blessed Trinity is One God in Three Persons. God is Father, Son, and Holy Spirit.

The Holy Spirit helps us to know that we are children of God the Father and brothers and sisters of Jesus. Jesus said to call God our Father, too. Jesus gave us the Lord's Prayer to lead us to his Father.

Praying the Lord's Prayer unites us with the Blessed Trinity. When we pray to God the Father, we pray in the name of Jesus by the power of the Holy Spirit.

 The Lord's Prayer

Activity

The Our Father and the Lord's Prayer are two names for the same prayer. Turn and talk to a friend about why you think there are two names. Circle your favorite name for the prayer.

Our Father | Lord's Prayer

Tell your friend or the group why you chose that name.

We honor God's name in the Lord's Prayer.

When we pray the Lord's Prayer, we honor and respect God's holy name. **Hallowed** is a word that means "holy." We also pray for the Kingdom of God. The **Kingdom of God** is the power of God's love in the world. When we pray for God's Kingdom to come, we are asking that all people will know and share God's love.

We also ask in the Lord's Prayer for God's will to be done. This means we want all things to happen everywhere just as God intends them.

When we pray the Lord's Prayer, we pray to God as our Father. We also remember that God is Father, Son, and Holy Spirit. We always praise the Blessed Trinity as One.

Faith Words

hallowed holy

Kingdom of God the power of God's love in the world

Activity

The word *hallowed* can mean "holy." Write *hallowed* where it belongs in the prayer below.

Our Father, who art in heaven,

_____ be thy name.

Color in God's name in the prayer. Talk with a friend about why God's name is holy.

We ask God for what we need.

God loves and cares for all people. Once when Jesus was teaching, some people were bringing children to see him. Some of his followers tried to keep the children away. Jesus said: "Let the children come to me and do not prevent them; for the kingdom of God belongs to such as these" (Luke 18:16).

Jesus loves all children. He wants them to know about his great love for them.

When we pray the Lord's Prayer, we show that we trust God's love and we trust him to care for us.

The Lord's Prayer	What we ask for ourselves
Give us this day our daily bread;	We ask God to give us what we need.
and forgive us our trespasses as we forgive those who trespass against us;	We ask God to forgive us. We need to forgive others.
and lead us not into temptation, but deliver us from evil.	We ask for help not to sin.

The Lord's Prayer is the perfect prayer. It is the prayer Jesus himself taught us. It brings us close to God the Father. It shows that we trust the help of the Holy Spirit. It shows that we want to live as Jesus taught.

Faith Words

hallowed   Kingdom of God

 Show What You Know

Match the terms to the correct definitions.

1. hallowed

2. Kingdom of God

3. the Our Father

another name for the Lord's Prayer

holy

the power of God's love in this world

Partners in Faith

Saint Damien of Molokai

Saint Damien of Molokai worked in Hawaii with very sick people whom others did not want to help. He was sad when he got sick himself. But he trusted God to help him.

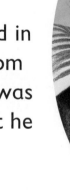 **Learn more about the life of Saint Damien of Molokai.**

Copyright © by William H. Sadlier, Inc. All rights reserved.

Mini-Task

We can call God by name every day in the Lord's Prayer. We praise God's name. We ask God to be in our lives.

Many people have day planners. They keep track of important things to do. Prayer should be an important part of each day.

Design a day for a planner. It can be a book or an app on a phone. Mark three times that are good to pray.

Share your design with a partner.

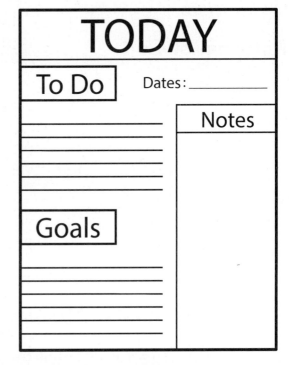

TODO

To Do   Dates: _____

Notes

Goals

 Want to do more? Go to your Portfolio to continue this activity.

At Home

Pray the Lord's Prayer every day this week with your family. Ask your family members about their favorite part of the prayer.

Copyright © by William H. Sadlier, Inc. All rights reserved.

Why and how do we celebrate the Church year?

Unit 5
Seasons and Feasts of the Church Year

DEC
JAN
FEB
MAR
APR
MAY
JUN
JUL
AUG
SEP
OCT
NOV
Advent
Christmas
Ordinary Time
Lent
Triduum
Easter
Ordinary Time
Liturgical Calendar

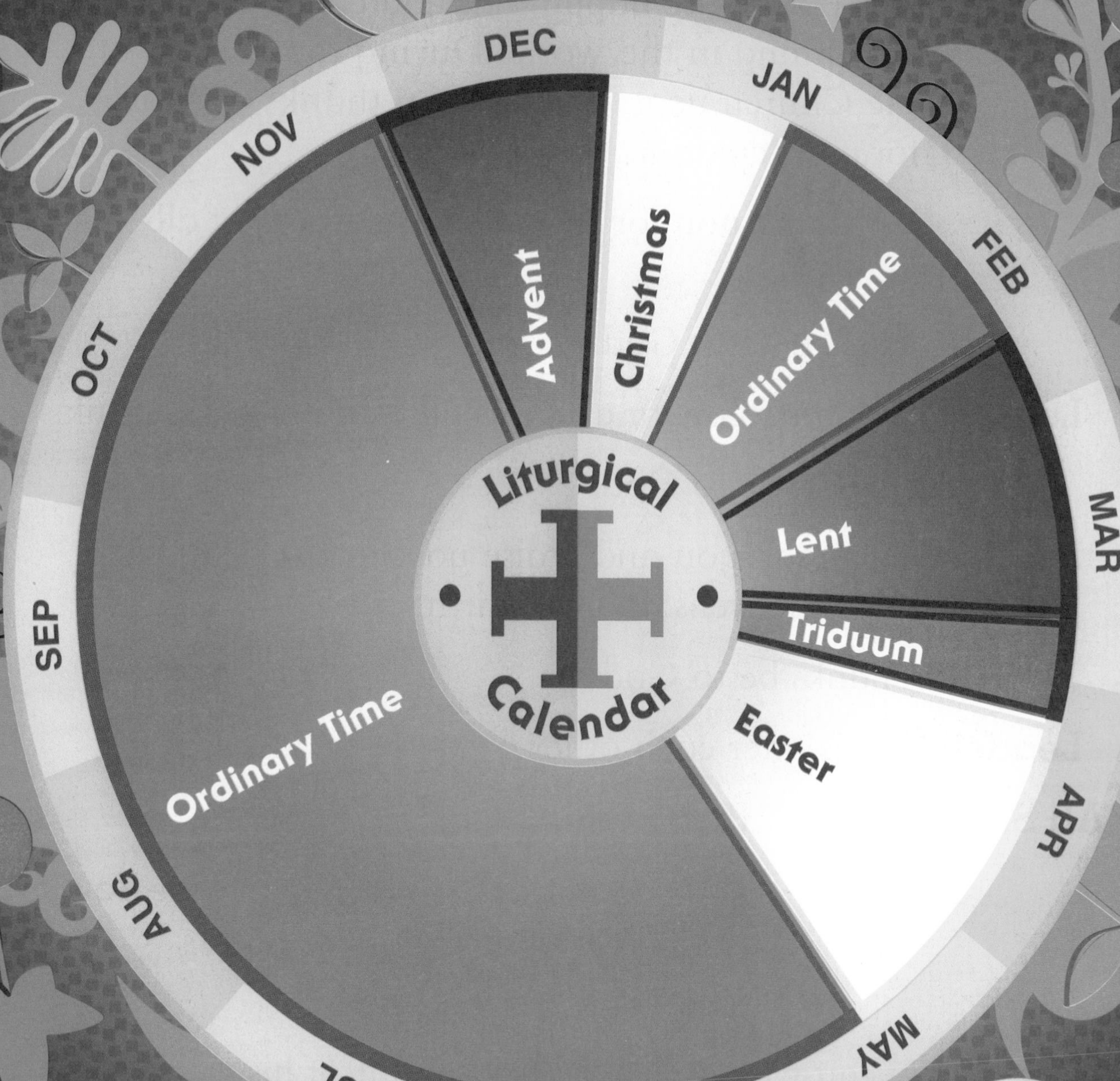

Unit Prayer

Leader: Saint Francis taught us to pray in different ways.

Let us listen to stories of missionary disciples who used all of creation to praise God.

Let us pray:
O God, we are happy that you created us and everything in the world. During the seasons of the Church year, we give you thanks at Mass for your creation.

We thank you for the earth, the home of all your people.

All: Thanks be to God.

Leader: We thank you for air to breathe and water to drink.

All: Thanks be to God.

Leader: We thank you and praise you for the beauty of the heavens and the earth.

All: Thanks be to God.

Leader: Let us offer each other a sign of peace.

All Sing: "We Will Praise You"

 Unit Song: "We Will Praise You," Tom Kendzia/OCP

Missionary Discipleship

How can we thank God for the gift of his creation? When did you know how much God loved you by giving us his creation?

How do we celebrate Jesus Christ?

Church Year

"I live by faith in the Son of God who has loved me." Galatians 2:20

 **Prayer**

Gathering Prayer

Leader: Let us praise God for the gift of his Son, Jesus. The Church helps us to know and love Jesus by giving us different feasts and seasons during the year. Together, let us say: "Glory and praise to you, O God."

All: (*bowing*) Glory and praise to you, O God.

Leader: Thank you for the seasons of Advent and Christmas to help us make room in our hearts for Jesus.

All: (*bowing*) Glory and praise to you, O God.

Leader: Thank you for the seasons of Lent and Easter when we remember Jesus' life, Death, and Resurrection in a special way.

All: (*bowing*) Glory and praise to you, O God.

Activity

Draw a picture of Jesus to share with others.

We celebrate Jesus as our Savior.

The Church year is also called the liturgical year. All through the year, we remember the life of Jesus. He is our Savior. Jesus shows us God the Father's love.

We celebrate Jesus' birth at Christmas. The season of Advent helps us prepare to welcome Jesus at Christmas.

We celebrate Jesus' Resurrection at Easter. The season of Lent prepares us to celebrate the suffering, Death, and Resurrection of Jesus. At Pentecost, we celebrate the Holy Spirit's presence in the Church. During Ordinary Time, we remember the life of Jesus. Jesus shows us the way to true happiness. He loves us and cares for us all year round.

Church Year

All through the Church year, the Church gathers to celebrate Mass every Sunday. Sunday is the day Jesus rose from the dead. We go to Mass on Sunday to worship God in prayer.

Did You Know?

 The Church year has many colors.

Activity

On which day do we celebrate Jesus' Resurrection?

_____

Talk in your group about what the Church does on this day to pray and celebrate.

Church Year Prayer Ritual

 "Open My Eyes," Jesse Manibusan/OCP

Leader: Let us celebrate the many ways that God loves us. We thank God for the seasons of the year: winter, spring, summer, and fall. We thank God for our family and friends.

When we are at Mass, we give thanks to God for all creation and give glory to his name.

Leader: Let us begin by blessing ourselves: "In the name of the Father, and of the Son, and of the Holy Spirit."

All: Amen!

Leader: When we say "Amen" at Mass or when praying, it means "Yes, I believe!"

Amen; yes, I believe.

All: Amen; yes, I believe.

Leader: We give glory and praise to God for all he has given us.

All: Amen; yes, I believe.

Leader: We praise God for the gift of his Son, Jesus.

All: Amen; yes, I believe.

Leader: We are created by God, and we thank him for the gift of life.

All: Amen; yes, I believe.

Leader: Let us each say one gift from God that makes us happy!

(All name a gift from God. After each gift, the leader prays:)

Leader: Thank you for your love for us.

Leader: At Mass, we give each other a sign of peace by shaking hands. Let us offer each other a sign of Christ's peace.

(All shake hands.)

Leader: O loving God, we believe that you are the Creator of all life. Let us say "Amen; yes, I believe."

All: Amen; yes, I believe.

How do I celebrate Jesus all year?

Mini-Task

As you learn about the seasons of the Church year, you are going to design trading cards. For each season, you will add a new card to your collection. You can keep your cards or trade cards with friends.

Complete this trading card for the Church year. Include a drawing of a way your family celebrates Jesus in your favorite season of the year. Show your trading card to your family. Tell about your drawing.

_____ celebrates the Church Year.

Name of season:

Color of season:

What we celebrate:

 Want to do more? Go to your Portfolio to continue this activity.

At Home

Talk as a family about your favorite seasons. Choose a way you can remember Jesus in every season.

Copyright © by William H. Sadlier, Inc. All rights reserved.

Why does Jesus come to save us?

Advent

"The people who walked in darkness have seen a great light." Isaiah 9:1

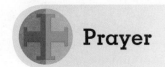 **Prayer**

Gathering Prayer

Leader: During Advent, let us prepare a place for Jesus in our hearts. As we pray before the Advent wreath, let the light of the four candles remind us of the light of Jesus that is born in our hearts. Help us to walk in your light, O Lord.

All: Help us to walk in your light, O Lord.

Leader: As we prepare our homes for Christmas, help us to prepare our hearts for your birth.

All: Help us to walk in your light, O Lord.

Leader: As we look for gifts for those we love, let us remember the gift of Jesus.

All: Help us to walk in your light, O Lord.

Activity

Color the Advent wreath as you pray this prayer:

Help us to walk in your light, O Lord.

Advent helps us prepare for the birth of Jesus.

When we plant a seed, we watch it grow. We know we must be patient. We are full of hope.

The season of Advent is a time to wait and hope. During Advent, we get ready to welcome Jesus into our hearts. Advent is four weeks long. We do things to get ready for Jesus. We pray. We help others. We learn more about our faith.

Little by little, our Advent time of waiting is filled with joy. When Christmas comes, we are ready to celebrate Jesus' birth. We welcome him into our hearts.

Advent

Did You Know?

  Waiting is a part of growing.

Activity

Circle the things you do to get ready every day.

What is something you can do to get ready for Jesus?

Readers Theater

The Announcement of the Birth of Jesus

Luke 1:26–38

Roles: Narrator 1, Narrator 2, Narrator 3, Narrator 4, Angel, Mary, All

The Angel Gabriel came to bring good news for Mary. Listen for the special message God sent to Mary.

Narrator 1: God sent an angel to the town of Nazareth.

Narrator 2: The angel was named Gabriel.

Narrator 3: The angel had good news for a woman named Mary.

Narrator 4: The Angel Gabriel spoke to Mary.

Angel: "Hail, favored one! The Lord is with you" (Luke 1:28).

Narrator 1: That means Mary was blessed in a special way.

Narrator 2: Mary was surprised that the Angel Gabriel came to her!

Angel: "Do not be afraid, Mary, for you have found favor with God" (Luke 1:30).

Narrator 3: The angel said Mary would have a baby.

Narrator 4: Her baby would be the Son of God.

Angel: You shall name the baby Jesus, and he will be great.

Mary: How can this be?

Angel: God has chosen you, Mary. "The child to be born will be called holy, the Son of God" (Luke 1:35).

Narrator 1: God knew that Mary was special.

Narrator 2: She would be the mother of Jesus, the Son of God.

Narrator 3: Mary was glad.

Narrator 4: The angel was glad.

Narrator 1: Then the Angel Gabriel was gone.

All: Everyone waited for Jesus to be born.

Why did Jesus come to save me?

Mini-Task

During the season of Advent, we get ready to celebrate the birth of Jesus.

You are going to design an Advent trading card. Think about the season and the ways you get ready for Jesus. Use words and pictures to design your card.

Show your trading card to a partner. Tell about your drawing.

_____ celebrates Advent.

Name of season:

Color of season:

What we celebrate:

 Want to do more? Go to your Portfolio to continue this activity.

At ome

As a family, think of all the kinds of light you have in your home. Some examples are lamps, sunlight through windows, candles, computers, and flashlights. Talk about why Jesus is the brightest light in your lives.

Copyright © by William H. Sadlier, Inc. All rights reserved.

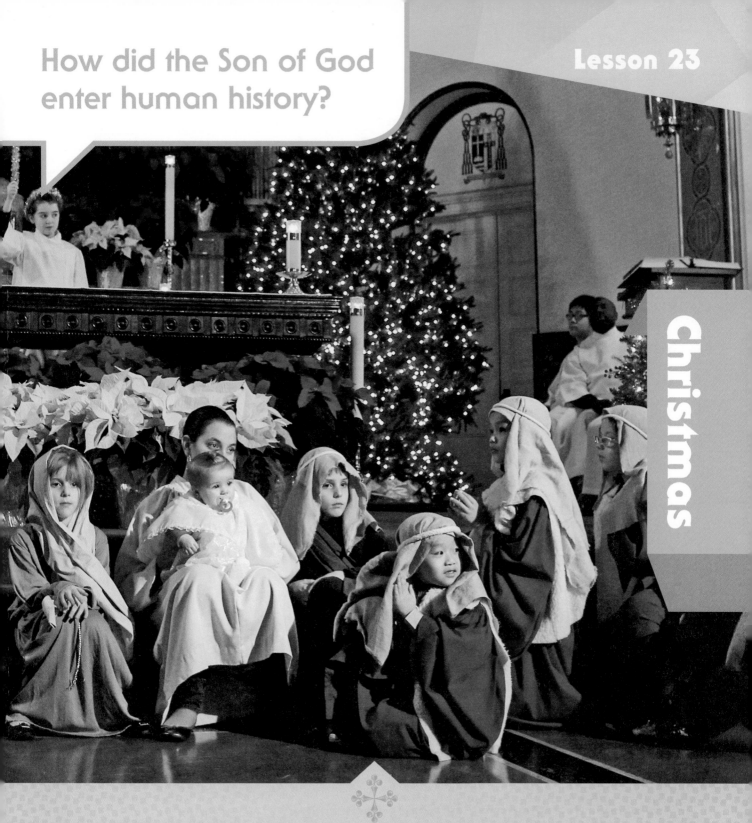

How did the Son of God enter human history?

Christmas

"For God so loved the world that he gave his only Son." John 3:16

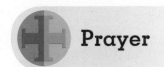 **Prayer**

Gathering Prayer

Leader: The joy of Christmas is God's greatest gift to the world: the birth of his Son, Jesus.

Glory to God in the highest!

All: Glory to God in the highest!

Leader: Jesus is the Light of the World, alive in our hearts.

All: Glory to God in the highest!

Leader: Jesus is the Prince of Peace, showing us how to live in peace with one another.

All: Glory to God in the highest!

Leader: Jesus is the Word of God, teaching us how to love God by the way we live.

All: Glory to God in the highest!

Activity

Look at the names of Jesus that are in the prayer. Circle the name you like best. Talk about why the name you chose is your favorite.

Light of the World   Prince of Peace   Word of God

Christmas is a season of love.

Christmas is a time of love. The most important gift of love at Christmas comes from God the Father. God loves us so much that he sent us his Son, Jesus. Jesus came to show us God the Father's love. He came to bring us joy.

Jesus was born in a stable. His mother, Mary, and her husband, Joseph, did not have many things. Yet they were happy. They loved Jesus. Their love shows us the love of God.

Christmas

Did You Know?

 The best gifts come from God.

Activity

Look at the picture of Jesus' birth. Draw lines from each person in the picture to the person's name.

Mary

Joseph

wise man

angel

Jesus

Readers Theater

The Birth of Jesus

Luke 2:8–20

Roles: Narrator 1, Narrator 2, Narrator 3, Narrator 4, Angel, Shepherd 1, Shepherd 2

The shepherds saw an angel who brought them good news. A baby was born, the Savior! They ran to see.

Narrator 1: Near the town of Bethlehem, shepherds were watching their sheep.

Narrator 2: It was night.

Narrator 3: It was very dark.

Narrator 4: The shepherds saw an angel!

Angel: I bring you "good news of great joy . . . . For today in the city of David a savior has been born" (Luke 2:10–11).

Narrator 1: The angel said they would find the Savior in a manger.

Narrator 2: The angel left.

Narrator 3: The angel went to heaven.

Narrator 4: The shepherds were amazed.

Shepherd 1: What can this be? Who is the Savior?

Shepherd 2: We must go to Bethlehem and see.

Narrator 1: The shepherds ran off to find Jesus.

Narrator 2: It did not take them long to see the manger.

Shepherd 1: Look! There is the baby, the Savior.

Shepherd 2: His mother and father are so happy!

Narrator 3: The shepherds told Mary and Joseph about the angel.

Narrator 4: Everyone was amazed by the story.

Shepherd 1: We must go back to our sheep now.

Shepherd 2: We must tell others about the Savior!

Narrator 1: Mary was happy with all that the shepherds said.

Narrator 2: The shepherds thanked God for letting them see the Savior.

How did Jesus come to us?

Mini-Task

During the season of Christmas, we celebrate God's gift of Jesus.

You are going to design a Christmas trading card. Think about the season and the ways we celebrate the birth of Jesus. Use words and pictures to design your card.

Show your trading card to a friend. Tell about your drawing.

_____

celebrates Christmas.

Name of season:

Color of season:

What we celebrate:

Want to do more? Go to your Portfolio to continue this activity.

At Home

Talk as a family about any Christmas traditions you have. Decide on a new tradition you can start to help you focus even more on Jesus this Christmas.

Copyright © by William H. Sadlier, Inc. All rights reserved.

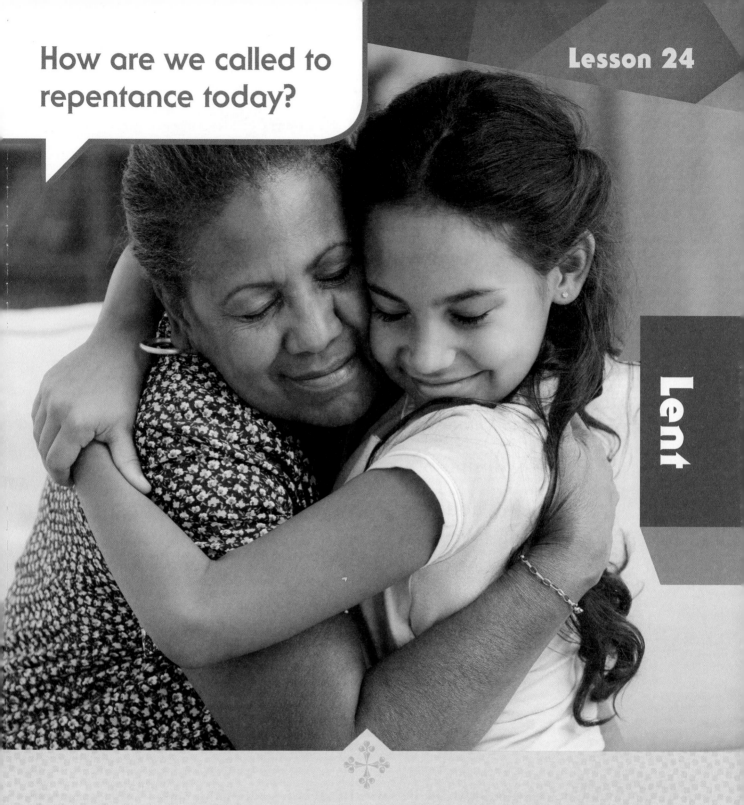

How are we called to repentance today?

Lent

"Faith, hope, love remain, these three; but the greatest of these is love."

1 Corinthians 13:13

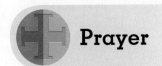 **Prayer**

Gathering Prayer

Leader: O God, in this season of Lent, help us to know more about the love that Jesus has given us. Thank you for sending Jesus to us.

(*Fold hands.*)

All: I will sing of your love forever.

Leader: O God, thank you for the joy in our hearts that is the love of Jesus.

(*Fold hands.*)

All: I will sing of your love forever.

Leader: Jesus, you showed your love for us in many ways. We remember you now with the Sign of the Cross.

All: In the name of the Father, and of the Son, and of the Holy Spirit. Amen.

Activity

What does Jesus give us in our hearts? Connect the dots to spell the answer.

Lent is a time to grow in love for God.

Lent is a time to grow. God helps us to grow in love. We show love in the things we do during Lent. We show love when we pray, when we thank Jesus for all he did for us, and when we help the poor.

One way to show love for God during Lent is through prayer. We can pray by ourselves, with our families, or with the whole Church. We can also do good things to help others. We can help those who are poor. To show our love for others, we give to the Church.

Lent is also a time to say we are sorry to God for times we did not follow his laws of love.

Lent

Did You Know?

 Ash Wednesday reminds us to love God more.

Activity

Work with a friend to make sentences about different ways we grow closer to God during Lent. Use the Word Bank to help you.

pray   **kind**   **love**   **chores**

Lent Prayer Ritual

 "Christ Be Our Light,"
Bernadette Farrell/OCP

Leader: Lent is a time for us to think about Jesus' love for us. God loves us so much that he gave us his Son. The Cross reminds us how much Jesus loved us. When we make the Sign of the Cross on ourselves, our whole body becomes a cross.

When each of us was baptized, the priest or deacon made the Sign of the Cross on our forehead, a sign that we were sealed in the love of the Father; his Son, Jesus; and the Holy Spirit. Let us come forward now to the water and make the Sign of the Cross on our foreheads.

Leader: Lord Jesus, help us see you in ourselves, in one another, and in the world.

Lord, have mercy.

All: Lord, have mercy.

Leader: Christ Jesus, help us thank you for always loving us.

Christ, have mercy.

All: Christ, have mercy.

Leader: Lord Jesus, help us to never forget how much you love us.

Lord, have mercy.

All: Lord, have mercy.

Leader: We will now pass a cross from one to another. As we do that, we will thank Jesus for his love.

(After all have held the cross and offered thanks, we pray:)

Leader: Let us fold our hands and close our eyes.

Lord, Jesus Christ, there is no greater love in the world than the love you have for us. By dying on the Cross, you gave of yourself to save us from our sins. Help us to remember this each time we make the Sign of the Cross.

In the name of the Father, and of the Son, and of the Holy Spirit. Amen.

Lent

How can I grow in love?

Mini-Task

The season of Lent is a time for us to grow closer to Jesus. During Lent, we think about everything Jesus did for us. We prepare ourselves for his Resurrection.

You are going to design a Lent trading card. Think about the season and the ways we prepare our hearts for Easter. Use words and pictures to design your card.

Show your trading card to your family. Tell about your drawing.

_____ celebrates Lent.

Name of season:

Color of season:

What we celebrate:

 Want to do more? Go to your Portfolio to continue this activity.

At Home

Have each family member name a way he or she has said "I love you" with actions or words.

Copyright © by William H. Sadlier, Inc. All rights reserved.

Why did Jesus die on the Cross and rise again?

Triduum

"By his wounds you have been healed."

1 Peter 2:24

Prayer

Gathering Prayer

Leader: Jesus, we remember how much you loved us by dying on the Cross. We know that you always love and forgive us. Praise to you, Lord Jesus Christ.

All: Praise to you, Lord Jesus Christ.

Leader: Jesus, you rose from the dead on Easter. With the angels in heaven, we pray: Alleluia, alleluia, praise to you, Lord Jesus Christ.

All: Alleluia, alleluia, praise to you, Lord Jesus Christ.

Leader: As we make the Sign of the Cross, help us to remember how much Jesus loves us. He gave his life for us on the Cross.

All: In the name of the Father, and of the Son, and of the Holy Spirit. Amen.

Activity

Work with a friend. Use the Word Bank to complete the prayer.

Lord   **Praise**   **Jesus**

_____ to you, _____ _____ Christ.

Teach the prayer to a family member.

We remember what Jesus did for us on three special days.

The Church celebrates three special days called the Triduum. The Triduum is the most important celebration of the Church's year. The days of the Triduum are Holy Thursday, Good Friday, and Easter Sunday and its vigil. Together, they tell about Jesus' Death and Resurrection.

Holy Thursday Before Jesus died on the Cross, he shared a special meal with his friends. It is called the Last Supper. We remember the Last Supper on Holy Thursday.

Good Friday On the Cross, Jesus showed his love by giving his life for us. He forgave those who hurt him. We remember Jesus' suffering on the Cross on Good Friday.

Easter Sunday On Easter, we remember that on the first Easter Sunday, God the Father raised Jesus from the dead! The Cross and the Resurrection are the greatest signs of God's love.

Did You Know?

 It is good to remember.

Activity

Match the things we remember to the correct day of the Triduum.

Holy Thursday	the Resurrection
Good Friday	the Last Supper
Easter Sunday	the Cross

Triduum Prayer Ritual

 "Take Up Your Cross," Jaime Cortez/OCP

Leader: In the name of the Father, and of the Son, and of the Holy Spirit. Amen.

Today we remember how much Jesus loves us. On Holy Thursday, Jesus shared a special meal with his friends. Jesus gave us his Body and Blood. We receive his Body and Blood in the Eucharist at Mass. On Good Friday, we remember that Jesus died on the Cross for us. On Holy Saturday, we quietly wait to celebrate Easter. Thank you, Jesus, for your love.

All: Thank you, Jesus, for your love.

Leader: We thank you, Jesus, for the gift of the Eucharist.

All: Thank you, Jesus, for your love.

Leader: We thank you, Jesus, for saving us from sin.

All: Thank you, Jesus, for your love.

Leader: We thank you, Jesus, for the light of your love.

All: Thank you, Jesus, for your love.

Leader: Let us offer our own prayers of thanks.

(*Silently say a prayer of thanks.*)

All: Thank you, Jesus.

Leader: Let us pray as Jesus taught us.
Our Father, who art in heaven,
hallowed be thy name;
thy kingdom come;
thy will be done on earth as it is in heaven.
Give us this day our daily bread;
and forgive us our trespasses,
as we forgive those who trespass against us;
and lead us not into temptation,
but deliver us from evil.
Amen.

Why did Jesus die on the Cross and rise again?

Mini-Task

In this lesson, you learned about the Triduum. The Triduum has three holy days. During the Triduum, we remember the Last Supper. We remember how Jesus died on the Cross and that he rose from the dead.

Design a Triduum trading card. Use words and pictures to design your card. Show your trading card to a partner. Tell about your drawing.

_____ celebrates the Triduum.

Name of season:

Color of season:

What we celebrate:

 Want to do more? Go to your Portfolio to continue this activity.

At Home

As a family, talk about ways you can celebrate the Triduum. If possible, go to church together for at least one of the Triduum liturgies.

Copyright © by William H. Sadlier, Inc. All rights reserved.

How is the Risen Jesus present in his Church?

Easter

"I am the resurrection and the life."

John 11:25

 **Prayer**

Gathering Prayer

Leader: We celebrate Easter, when Jesus rose from the dead. Let us live in the light of the Risen Lord. Sing "Alleluia," for Christ is alive!

All: Forever we will sing "Alleluia."

Leader: Christ Jesus, your Death on a Cross was not the end for you. And because of your Resurrection, we will live with you forever!

All: Forever we will sing "Alleluia."

Leader: Lord Jesus, our hearts are filled with love. It is the love of your light in us.

All: Forever we will sing "Alleluia."

Leader: We share the light of the Risen Jesus with our families and friends.

All: Forever we will sing "Alleluia."

Activity

Unscramble the word to complete the sentence.

elvo

We share the _____ of Jesus at Easter.

Tell a friend one way we do this.

God fills our hearts with Easter joy.

The Easter season lasts for fifty days. It begins on Easter Sunday. During the Easter season, we are glad because Jesus is risen. We sing "Alleluia!" to show our joy. The priest wears white vestments. White is the Easter color.

A special Paschal candle is blessed during the Triduum at the Easter Vigil. All through the season, this candle is lighted. The candle reminds us of Jesus. He is the Light of the World.

We give thanks to God because Jesus is risen. We decorate the church with plants to remind us of new life. Easter is a joyful time.

Did You Know?

 Creation is a part of the Easter celebration.

Activity

Decorate the Paschal candle. Draw the symbols and write the year on your candle.

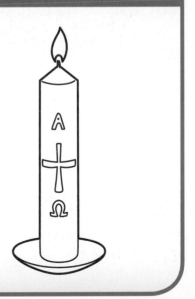

Readers Theater

Jesus Is Risen!

Matthew 28:1–10

Roles: Narrator 1, Narrator 2, Narrator 3, Narrator 4, Angel, Jesus

Mary Magdalene and another Mary have good news to share.

Narrator 1: Mary Magdalene and another Mary went to the tomb of Jesus.

Narrator 2: They wanted to visit the place where Jesus was buried.

Narrator 3: Suddenly, the earth shook!

Narrator 4: An angel came from heaven.

Narrator 1: The angel rolled back the stone from the tomb.

Angel: "Do not be afraid!" (Matthew 28:5)

Narrator 2: The angel knew they were looking for Jesus.

Narrator 3: The angel said to Mary Magdalene and the other Mary:

Angel: "[Jesus] is not here, for he has been raised just as he said" (Matthew 28:6).

Narrator 4: Mary Magdalene and Mary looked into the tomb. Jesus was not there.

Narrator 1: They ran to tell the other disciples what happened.

Narrator 2: Mary Magdalene and Mary met someone on their way home. It was Jesus!

Narrator 3: They knelt before Jesus.

Jesus: "Do not be afraid. Go tell my brothers to go to Galilee, and there they will see me" (Matthew 28:10).

Narrator 4: Mary Magdalene and the other Mary were so happy!

Narrator 1: They ran to tell the other disciples the good news about Jesus.

All: Jesus is risen from the dead!

How is the Risen Jesus present in his Church?

Mini-Task

At Easter, we remember that Jesus' Resurrection means that we, too, can live forever with God in heaven.

As you plan your trading card, think about the ways we celebrate Easter. Use words and pictures in your trading card.

Show your trading card to a friend. Tell about your drawing.

_____

celebrates Easter.

Name of season:

Color of season:

What we celebrate:

Want to do more? Go to your Portfolio to continue this activity.

At Home

Ask family members what they would have said to Jesus if they had been there with the women at the empty tomb.

Copyright © by William H. Sadlier, Inc. All rights reserved.

Who is the Holy Spirit?

Pentecost

"The Spirit of truth . . . will be in you."

John 14:17

 **Prayer**

Gathering Prayer

Leader: At Pentecost, we celebrate the Gift of the Holy Spirit. On that day, the disciples were filled with the Holy Spirit. They were given courage and strength.

The Holy Spirit sent the disciples into the world to teach about Jesus. We, too, are disciples of Jesus. We will share the Good News about Jesus!

All: We will share the Good News about Jesus!

Leader: We are filled with the Holy Spirit. Let us be a sign of love in the world.

All: We will share the Good News about Jesus!

Leader: We are filled with the Holy Spirit. Let us be a sign of peace in the world.

All: We will share the Good News about Jesus!

Leader: We are filled with the Holy Spirit. Let us share the Good News of Jesus with the world.

All: We will share the Good News about Jesus!

Activity

Talk with a friend about how you can be a sign of God's love in the world. Act out your idea for the rest of your group.

The Church was revealed at Pentecost.

After Jesus ascended into heaven, he sent the Holy Spirit. The Easter season ends on Pentecost Sunday. At the first Pentecost, the Apostles and Mary were praying. They heard a loud noise and felt a strong wind. A small flame appeared over each of them. The Holy Spirit was with them.

The Holy Spirit fills our hearts with joy and love today, too. The Holy Spirit makes us strong and helps us to share the Good News of Jesus.

On Pentecost, the church is decorated in red to remind us of the fire of the Holy Spirit. We pray for the Holy Spirit to make us strong and to fill our hearts with love.

Did You Know?

 Sharing is caring.

Activity

Color the flames above the Apostles' heads.

Next, color the rest of the picture.

Then turn and talk to a friend about what is happening in the picture.

Readers Theater

The Holy Spirit Comes

Acts of the Apostles 2:1–13

Roles: Narrator 1, Narrator 2, Narrator 3, Narrator 4, Disciple 1, Disciple 2

Jesus sends the Holy Spirit to the disciples.

Narrator 1: Jesus had gone to heaven.

Narrator 2: The disciples were afraid.

Narrator 3: They were together in a big room.

Narrator 4: They did not know what to do.

Disciple 1: What is that loud noise?

Disciple 2: I can hear the noise everywhere!

Narrator 1: The loud noise was the Holy Spirit.

Narrator 2: Jesus had sent his Spirit to the disciples.

Narrator 3: Tongues of fire came on top of the disciples' heads.

Disciple 1: Look at the fire!

Disciple 2: What is the fire?

Narrator 4: The disciples "were all filled with the holy Spirit" (Acts of the Apostles 2:4).

Narrator 1: The Holy Spirit gave them courage.

Narrator 2: The disciples wanted to share the Good News.

Disciple 1: I want to tell the world about Jesus!

Disciple 2: We will go outside and tell all the people.

Narrator 3: The Holy Spirit made the disciples strong.

Narrator 4: They were not afraid anymore.

Narrator 1: The disciples would tell the whole world about Jesus!

Who is the Holy Spirit?

Mini-Task

During Pentecost, we celebrate the Gift of the Holy Spirit. We remember the day that the disciples were filled with the Holy Spirit.

Remember the first Pentecost. Think about the ways we celebrate today. Use words and pictures on your trading card.

Tell a friend about your trading card.

_____ celebrates Pentecost.

Name of season:

Color of season:

What we celebrate:

 Want to do more? Go to your Portfolio to continue this activity.

 At Home

As a family, hold hands in prayer before bedtime or a meal. Feel the warmth of your hands. Talk about how the Holy Spirit warmed the hearts of the disciples and can warm our hearts, too.

Copyright © by William H. Sadlier, Inc. All rights reserved.

How do we grow as Jesus' followers?

Ordinary Time

"Jesus Christ is the same yesterday, today, and forever." Hebrews 13:8

Gathering Prayer

Leader: We praise you, O God, for the season of Ordinary Time.

Jesus wants us to follow him. In Ordinary Time, we hear the stories of how Jesus called people to him from the very beginning of his work in the world.

We hear your call and follow you, O Lord.

All: We hear your call and follow you, O Lord.

Leader: We listen to the stories of your life and work. We pray and learn from you.

All: We hear your call and follow you, O Lord.

Leader: We know that we are your disciples, too. We do your work in the world.

All: We hear your call and follow you, O Lord.

Activity

In Ordinary Time, we hear stories of Jesus' life and work. Tell a friend a story you know about Jesus.

We can do good things for God.

During Ordinary Time, the Church tells us stories about Jesus and his followers. At Mass, the priest wears green. Green is the color of hope and growth.

We hear about how Jesus called his first followers. They were fishermen. When he called them, they followed him. They were the first Church.

Jesus called other people, too, and they followed him as well. They traveled with Jesus from town to town.

Jesus healed the sick and taught his followers to love one another. He said that everyone could enter God's Kingdom of peace and joy. In God's Kingdom, we can be friends with God and one another.

During Ordinary Time, we listen to the teachings of Jesus. We hear about the wonderful things he did. We grow in faith and learn about God's Kingdom.

Ordinary Time

Did You Know?

 Ordinary can be great.

Activity

Imagine that you lived in the time of Jesus. What would you say if Jesus called you to follow him? Talk with friends about things you could say or do.

Ordinary Time Prayer Ritual

 "Wade in the Water," Spiritual

Leader: Let us pray: In the name of the Father, and of the Son, and of the Holy Spirit. Amen.

Jesus taught his followers by telling stories. Most of us love to listen to stories. Jesus knew that people would learn about God the Father through stories. Spread out your arms to accept Jesus as we say: "Speak, Lord; I am listening."

All: Speak, Lord; I am listening.

Leader: Jesus said: "Love one another as I love you" (John 15:12).

All: Speak, Lord; I am listening.

Leader: Jesus said: "I am the resurrection and the life; whoever believes in me . . . will live [forever]" (John 11:25).

All: Speak, Lord; I am listening.

Leader: We pray for the pope and the leaders of the Church, that they hear God's Word.

All: Speak, Lord; I am listening.

Leader: We pray for our parish, that we listen to God's Word and follow him.

All: Speak, Lord; I am listening.

Leader: We pray for our families that God's Word will be alive in our homes.

All: Speak, Lord; I am listening.

Leader: We pray for one another that we see the love of God here in us.

All: Speak, Lord; I am listening.

Leader: We will offer each other a sign of Christ's peace.

(Offer each other a handshake as a sign of Christ's peace.)

Leader: Speak, Lord; I am listening!

How do we grow as Jesus' followers?

Mini-Task

During the season of Ordinary Time, we remember all the good things Jesus did for us. Ordinary Time helps us learn how to be followers of Jesus.

What do you think is most important about Ordinary Time? Use words and pictures to design a trading card.

Show your trading card to your family. Tell about your drawing.

_____

celebrates Ordinary Time.

Name of season:

Color of season:

What we celebrate:

 **Want to do more? Go to your Portfolio to continue this activity.**

At Home

Talk with your family members about ways you can be better listeners. Pray together silently. Listen for what God may be saying to each of you.

Copyright © by William H. Sadlier, Inc. All rights reserved.

Welcome

to your *Christ In Us* Sourcebook

Sign of the Cross

In the name of the Father,
and of the Son,
and of the Holy Spirit.
Amen.

Our Father

Our Father, who art in heaven,
hallowed be thy name;
thy kingdom come;
thy will be done on earth as
      it is in heaven.
Give us this day our daily bread;
and forgive us our trespasses
as we forgive those who
      trespass against us;
and lead us not into
temptation,
but deliver us from evil.
Amen.

Hail Mary

Hail Mary, full of grace,
the Lord is with you!
Blessed are you among women,
and blessed is the fruit of
      your womb, Jesus.
Holy Mary, Mother of God,
pray for us sinners,
now and at the hour of our death.
Amen.

Glory Be to the Father

Glory be to the Father
and to the Son
and to the Holy Spirit,
as it was in the beginning,
is now, and ever shall be
world without end.
Amen.

Grace Before Meals

Bless us, O Lord,
      and these your gifts
which we are about to receive
from your goodness.
Through Christ our Lord.
Amen.

Grace After Meals

We give you thanks, almighty God,
for these and all your gifts,
which we have received through
Christ our Lord.
Amen.

Jesus Prayer

Lord Jesus Christ,
Son of God, have mercy on me,
a sinner.

Act of Contrition

My God,
I am sorry for my sins with
    all my heart.
In choosing to do wrong
and failing to do good,
I have sinned against you
whom I should love above
    all things.
I firmly intend, with your help,
to do penance,
to sin no more,
and to avoid whatever
    leads me to sin.
Our Savior Jesus Christ
suffered and died for us.
In his name, my God, have mercy.
Amen.

Angel of God

Angel of God,
my guardian dear,
to whom God's love commits
    me here,
ever this day be at my side,
to light and guard, to rule and
    guide.

Apostles' Creed

I believe in God, the Father almighty,
    Creator of heaven and earth,
and in Jesus Christ, his only Son,
    our Lord,
who was conceived by the Holy Spirit,
born of the Virgin Mary,
suffered under Pontius Pilate,
was crucified, died and was buried;
he descended into hell;
on the third day he rose again
from the dead;
he ascended into heaven,
and is seated at the right hand
    of God the Father almighty;
from there he will come to judge
    the living and the dead.
I believe in the Holy Spirit,
    the holy Catholic Church,
    the communion of saints,
    the forgiveness of sins,
    the resurrection of the body,
    and life everlasting. Amen.

Prayer Before the Blessed Sacrament

Jesus,
You are God-with-us,
especially in this Sacrament of the
 Eucharist.
You love me as I am and help me to grow.
Come and be with me in all my joys
 and sorrows.
Help me share your peace and
love with everyone I meet.
I ask in your name.
Amen.

Morning Offering

My God, I offer you today
all that I think and do
 and say,
uniting it with what
 was done
on earth, by Jesus Christ,
your son.

Evening Prayer

Dear God, before I sleep
I want to thank you for
 this day
so full of your kindness
and your joy,
I close my eyes to rest
safe in your loving care.

Act of Faith

Oh God, we believe in all that Jesus has
 taught us about you.
We place all our trust in you
 because of your great love for us.

Act of Hope

Oh God, we never give up on your love.
We have hope and will work for your
Kingdom to come and for a life that
 lasts forever with you in heaven.

Act of Love

Oh God, we love you above all things.
Help us to love ourselves and one
 another as Jesus taught us to do.

The Rosary

Praying the Rosary creates a peaceful rhythm of prayer during which we can reflect on the Mysteries of the Rosary, special times in the lives of Jesus and Mary. Follow the numbered steps to pray the Rosary.

5. Pray the Glory Be to the Father after each set of small beads.

End

6. Pray the Hail Holy Queen to end the Rosary.

4. Pray a Hail Mary at every small bead.

3. Pray an Our Father at every large bead.

2. Then pray the Apostles' Creed.

1. Start with the Sign of the Cross.

Start

1. **sanctuary** the part of the church that includes the altar and the ambo. The word *sanctuary* means "holy place."

2. **altar** the special table that is the center of the celebration of the Liturgy of the Eucharist, also called the Table of the Lord

3. **crucifix** a cross in the sanctuary with a figure of Christ crucified

4. **tabernacle** the special place in the church in which the Most Blessed Sacrament is placed in reserve

5. **sanctuary lamp** light or candle that is always lit near the tabernacle. It helps us to remember that Jesus is really present in the Most Blessed Sacrament.

6. **ambo** a sacred reading stand called the Table of the Word of God. The ambo is used only for proclamation of the Scripture in the Liturgy.

7. **chalice** the special cup into which the priest pours grape wine that becomes the Blood of Christ during the Liturgy of the Eucharist

8. **paten** the special plate on which the priest places the wheat bread that becomes the Body of Christ during the Liturgy of the Eucharist

9. **cruets** small glass jars that contain the water and the grape wine used at Mass

10. **presider's chair** chair on which the priest who is celebrating Mass sits

11 **processional cross** cross with a figure of Christ crucified that is carried in the entrance procession and may also be carried during the Offertory procession and during recessional

12 **Paschal candle** a large candle that is blessed and lit every Easter. The lighted Paschal candle represents the Risen Christ among us. The flame of the Paschal candle is used to light baptismal candles.

13 **baptismal font or pool** contains the water that is blessed and used during the Sacrament of Baptism

14 **Stations of the Cross** fourteen pictures that help us to follow the footsteps of Jesus during his Passion and Death on the Cross

15 **Reconciliation Room or confessional** a separate space for celebrating the Sacrament of Penance and Reconciliation. This is where you meet the priest for individual confession and absolution. You may sit and talk to him face-to-face or kneel behind a screen.

16 **stained glass** colorful windows that may show saints or scenes from Scripture

17 **pews** where the assembly is seated during the celebration of Mass

18 **statue of Mary** image of the Mother of God, our greatest saint. Statues of other saints may also be found in the church.

The Ten Commandments

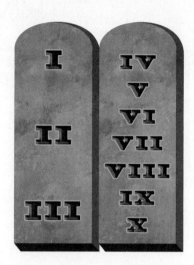

1. I am the LORD your God: you shall not have strange gods before me.
2. You shall not take the name of the LORD your God in vain.
3. Remember to keep holy the LORD's Day.
4. Honor your father and your mother.
5. You shall not kill.
6. You shall not commit adultery.
7. You shall not steal.
8. You shall not bear false witness against your neighbor.
9. You shall not covet your neighbor's wife.
10. You shall not covet your neighbor's goods.

The Seven Sacraments

Baptism
Eucharist
Penance and Reconciliation
Confirmation
Matrimony
Holy Orders
Anointing of the Sick

Stations of the Cross

In the Stations of the Cross, we follow in the footsteps of Jesus during his Passion and Death on the cross.

1 Jesus is condemned to die.

2 Jesus takes up his cross.

3 Jesus falls the first time.

4 Jesus meets his mother.

5 Simon helps Jesus carry his cross.

6 Veronica wipes the face of Jesus.

7 Jesus falls the second time.

8 Jesus meets the women of Jerusalem.

9 Jesus falls the third time.

10 Jesus is stripped of his garments.

11 Jesus is nailed to the cross.

12 Jesus dies on the cross.

13 Jesus is taken down from the cross.

14 Jesus is laid in the tomb.

Holy Water

Holy water is water that has been blessed. A holy water font containing that blessed water is placed near the door of the church. When we enter the church, we put our fingers into the holy water and then make the Sign of the Cross. The water reminds us of our Baptism.

Baptismal Font

Every parish church has a baptismal font. It is the vessel that holds the holy water used for the Sacrament of Baptism. Some fonts are simple, and some are large and ornate.

Holy Places

We treat places of prayer (churches, synagogues, temples, and mosques) with reverence. In our Catholic churches, we genuflect toward the tabernacle as we enter our pew. Genuflecting (touching our right knee to the floor) is a sign of our reverence for Jesus Christ, who is really present in the Blessed Sacrament.

The Holy Family

Jesus is God the Son who became one of us. He grew up in a family. Jesus prayed every morning and every night with his mother, Mary, and his foster father, Joseph. Jesus' family showed their love for God and one another. All families should try to be like the Holy Family!

Holy Days of Obligation

Solemnity of Mary, Mother of God (January 1)

Ascension (when celebrated on Thursday during the Easter season*)

Assumption of Mary (August 15)

All Saints' Day (November 1)

Immaculate Conception (December 8)

Christmas (December 25)

Some dioceses celebrate the Ascension on the following Sunday.

249

A Roadmap to Happiness: The Beatitudes

What makes your family happy? When we live as Jesus' disciples, we can find true happiness. The Beatitudes are Jesus' teachings that describe the way to live as disciples. In the Beatitudes, the word *blessed* means "happy."

The Beatitudes

✢ "Blessed are the poor in spirit,
     for theirs is the kingdom
        of heaven.

✢ Blessed are they who mourn,
     for they will be comforted.

✢ Blessed are the meek,
     for they will inherit the land.

✢ Blessed are they who hunger
     and thirst for righteousness,
        for they will be satisfied.

✢ Blessed are the merciful,
     for they will be shown mercy.

✢ Blessed are the clean of heart,
     for they will see God.

✢ Blessed are the peacemakers, for
     they will be called children
        of God.

✢ Blessed are they who are persecuted
     for the sake of righteousness,
        for theirs is the kingdom of heaven." Matthew 5:3–10

Your *Christ In Us*

Family Companion

Welcome. We are so glad that you are a *Christ In Us* family. In this section, you will find a treasury of resources as your family accompanies your child on our journey to a greater love in Jesus Christ. This material is written specifically for you as adult family members. But be certain that you review your child's resources that precede this section. Also, don't forget to look over the *Glossary* that follows. It will give you a good overview of what your child has been experiencing this year. Finally, the *Q&A* offers a wonderful opportunity for your entire family to review the major faith statements of the grade.

The Holy Spirit, Third Person of the Blessed Trinity

Share memories, pictures, or keepsakes of your child's Baptism. Explain that we all receive the gifts of the Holy Spirit at our Baptism. The Holy Spirit is always present with the Father and the Son. Jesus promised to send the Holy Spirit to strengthen and support his followers. The Holy Spirit still guides the Church. In the Nicene Creed, we express our belief in the Holy Spirit. Pray the Creed and note the parts that refer to the Holy Spirit. Also, pray the Prayer to the Holy Spirit together.

Nicene Creed

I believe in one God,
   the Father almighty,
   maker of heaven and earth,
   of all things visible and invisible.

I believe in one Lord Jesus Christ,
   the Only Begotten Son of God,
   born of the Father before all ages.
   God from God, Light from Light,
   true God from true God,
   begotten, not made, consubstantial
     with the Father;
   through him all things were made.
   For us men and for our salvation
     he came down from heaven,
   and by the Holy Spirit
     was incarnate of the Virgin Mary,
     and became man.

For our sake he was crucified
     under Pontius Pilate,
   he suffered death and was buried,
   and rose again on the third day
     in accordance with the Scriptures.
   He ascended into heaven
     and is seated at the right hand
     of the Father.
   He will come again in glory to judge
     the living and the dead
     and his kingdom will have no end.
I believe in the Holy Spirit, the Lord,
   the giver of life,

who proceeds from the Father and the Son,
   who with the Father and the Son is
     adored and glorified,
   who has spoken through the prophets.

I believe in one, holy, catholic
   and apostolic Church.
I confess one Baptism for
   the forgiveness of sins
and I look forward to the resurrection of the dead
     and the life of the world to come. Amen.

Prayer to the Holy Spirit

Come, Holy Spirit, fill the heart of your faithful.
And kindle in them the fire of your love.
Send forth your spirit and they shall be created.
And you will renew the face of the earth.

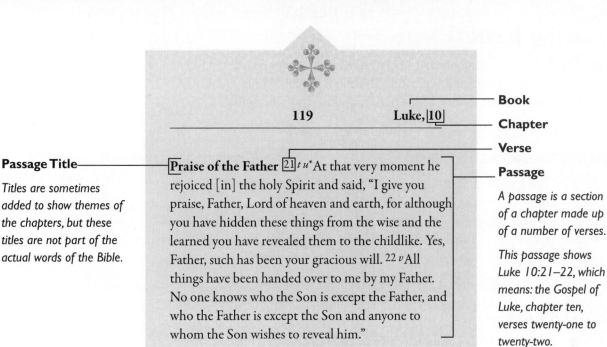

119   Luke, |10|

Book

Chapter

Verse

Passage

Passage Title

Titles are sometimes added to show themes of the chapters, but these titles are not part of the actual words of the Bible.

Praise of the Father |21| *t u**At that very moment he rejoiced [in] the holy Spirit and said, "I give you praise, Father, Lord of heaven and earth, for although you have hidden these things from the wise and the learned you have revealed them to the childlike. Yes, Father, such has been your gracious will. ²² *v*All things have been handed over to me by my Father. No one knows who the Son is except the Father, and who the Father is except the Son and anyone to whom the Son wishes to reveal him."

A passage is a section of a chapter made up of a number of verses.

This passage shows Luke 10:21–22, which means: the Gospel of Luke, chapter ten, verses twenty-one to twenty-two.

Reading the Bible . . . in Five Easy Steps

When you are given a Scripture passage to read, here are five easy steps that will help you to find it! With your child, follow these steps to look up **Lk 10:21–22**.

1. **Find the book.** When the name of the book is abbreviated, locate the meaning of the abbreviation on the contents pages at the beginning of your Bible. *Lk* stands for *Luke*, one of the four Gospels.

2. **Find the page.** Your Bible's contents pages will also show the page on which the book begins. Turn to that page within your Bible.

3. **Find the chapter.** Once you arrive at the page where the book begins, keep turning the pages forward until you find the right chapter. The image above shows you how a chapter number is usually displayed on a typical Bible page. You are looking for chapter **10** in Luke.

4. **Find the verses.** Once you find the right chapter, locate the verse or verses you need within the chapter. The image above also shows you how verse numbers will look on a typical Bible page. You are looking for verses **21** and **22**.

5. **Start reading!**

Following Jesus

Jesus gave us two commandments that help us live like him. Read and talk about these commandments as a family. Let them guide all your relationships—at home, at school, in the parish, and in the community.

Great Commandment

"You shall love the Lord, your God, with all your heart, with all your soul, and with all your mind. This is the greatest and the first commandment. The second is like it: You shall love your neighbor as yourself." (Matthew 22:37-39)

New Commandment

"I give you a new commandment: love one another. As I have loved you, so you also should love one another. This is how all will know that you are my disciples, if you have love for one another." (John 13:34-35)

Peace and Justice

As disciples of Jesus we must commit to justice and become peacemakers in every context of our lives. Justice is based on the simple fact that all people have human dignity, the value and worth we share because God created us in his image and likeness. In Scripture, we find that God's peace, which is more than just the absence of war and violence, is realized when everyone lives in true harmony with one another and with God's creation.

"The work of justice will be peace; the effect of justice, calm and security forever."

Isaiah 32:17

Talk to your child about what it means to treat others justly.

Prayer of Saint Francis

Lord, make me an instrument of your peace:
where there is hatred let me sow love;
where there is injury, pardon;
where there is doubt, faith;
where there is despair, hope;
where there is darkness, light;
where there is sadness, joy.

O divine Master, grant that I may not so
    much seek
to be consoled as to console,
to be understood as to understand,
to be loved as to love.
For it is in giving that we receive,
it is in pardoning that we are pardoned,
it is in dying that we are born to eternal life.
Amen.

Praying with Mary

Jesus loved and honored his mother. The Church has always loved and honored Mary. Mary trusted God completely. When asked to be the mother of God's Son, she said: "May it be done to me according to your word" (Luke 1:38).

The Angelus is a devotion that celebrates the Incarnation and Mary's role in our salvation. The Angelus is prayed three times a day: morning, noon, and evening.

The Angelus

The angel spoke God's message to Mary,
and she conceived of the Holy Spirit.
Hail Mary…
"I am the lowly servant of the Lord:
let it be done to me according to you word."
Hail Mary…
And the Word became flesh
and lived among us.
Hail Mary…
Pray for us, holy Mother of God,
that we may be made worthy of the
    promises of Christ.
Let us pray.
Lord,
fill our hearts with your grace:
once through the message of an angel
you revealed to us the Incarnation of your Son;
now, through his suffering and death
lead us to the glory of his resurrection.
We ask this through Christ our Lord.
Amen.

AVE·GRATIA·PLENA·DOMINUS·TECUM.

The Power of Grace

How do we live as disciples of Jesus? Through the power of God's grace, we can grow in friendship with God. Grace is a share in God's life and love. We receive grace at our Baptism and when we receive the other sacraments. Throughout our lives, grace helps us respond to God with love. It gives us strength to live as Jesus' disciples.

Messengers of God

Aside from honoring Mary and the saints in prayer, we can also call on God's angels in prayer. Angels are creatures created by God as pure spirits. They do not have physical bodies. They serve God in his saving plan for us and constantly give him praise. Everyone has a guardian angel. We also recognize the Archangels Michael, Raphael, and Gabriel for their special roles as God's messengers in the Bible. We can ask the angels to help us in living as disciples of Jesus.

Prayer to Saint Michael the Archangel

Saint Michael the Archangel,
defend us in battle.
Be our defense against the wickedness
    and snares of the Devil.
May God rebuke him, we humbly pray, and
    do thou,
O Prince of the heavenly hosts,
by the power of God,
thrust into hell Satan,
and all the evil spirits,
who prowl about the world
seeking the ruin of souls. Amen.

Glossary

angel (page 44) an invisible being that is a messenger of God

Anointing of the Sick (page 90) the sacrament in which the priest prays for the Holy Spirit to bring God's comfort and peace to those who are sick

Apostles (page 56) twelve men Jesus chose to lead his followers

Baptism (page 79) the first sacrament we receive, which gives us new life in Jesus

Beatitudes (page 134) teachings of Jesus that describe the way to live as his followers

Bible (page 21) the Church's holy book of God's Word

bishops (page 56) leaders of the Church who continue the work of the Apostles

Blessed Trinity (page 29) One God in Three Persons: God the Father, God the Son, and God the Holy Spirit

blessing (page 74) a prayer that asks God to make someone or something holy

Christ (page 46) a name for Jesus that means "the chosen one of God"

Church (page 24) all the people who are baptized in the name of the Blessed Trinity and are part of the Body of Christ

commandments (page 107) laws that God gave us

Confirmation (page 81) the sacrament that strengthens us with the Gift of the Holy Spirit

creation (page 28) everything God made out of nothing

deacons (page 56) men who serve the Church by assisting priests and bishops

devotion (page 74) a form of personal or communal prayer

Eucharist (page 82) the sacrament of the Body and Blood of Jesus Christ

faith (page 37) a gift from God that helps us to believe in him

grace (page 80) God's life in us

Great Commandment (page 108) Jesus' teaching to love God, ourselves, and others

hallowed (page 180) holy

heaven (page 48) life with God forever

Holy Family (page 97) the family of Jesus, Mary, and Joseph

Holy Orders (page 96) the sacrament in which a baptized man becomes a deacon, a priest, or a bishop

invite (page 149) to ask someone to do something

just (page 116) fair

Kingdom of God (page 180) the power of God's love in the world

Last Supper (page 82) the meal that Jesus shared with his followers on the night before he died

liturgy (page 64) the work and prayer of the whole Church

Lord's Prayer (page 165) the prayer Jesus taught his followers

Mass (page 70) the Church's most important celebration

Matrimony (page 96) the sacrament in which a baptized man and a baptized woman become husband and wife

mercy (page 140) God's love and forgiveness

Original Sin (page 128) The first sin. It was committed when the first man and woman, Adam and Eve, disobeyed God.

parish (page 71) a community within the Church that worships God together

Penance and Reconciliation (page 89) the sacrament in which we receive and celebrate God's forgiveness

People of God (page 52) another name for the Church

praise (page 154) prayer that shows respect for God and his greatness

prayer (page 62) listening to and talking with God

priests (page 56) men who serve the Church by teaching and leading our prayers

sacraments (page 65) special signs Jesus gave to the Church to share God's life and love with us

sacramentals (page 66) blessings, actions, and objects that help us live holy lives

saints (page 72) followers of Jesus who led holy lives and now live happily forever with God in heaven

sin (page 88) any thought, word, or action that we do on purpose even though we know that it is wrong

Ten Commandments (page 120) ten special laws God gave to his people

unite (page 173) to bring together

virtue (page 115) a good habit that helps us act as God wants us to

worship (page 71) adoration and honor given to God in prayer

Q&A

Q: What is the Bible?

A: The Bible is the Church's book of God's Word. *CCC, 136*

Q: What is the Church?

A: The Church is all the people who are baptized in the name of the Blessed Trinity and are part of the Body of Christ. The Church is like a family that wants to know and love God together. Jesus is the head of the family. Jesus gives us the Church to unite us all with him. *CCC, 807, 810*

Q: What is creation?

A: Creation is everything God made out of nothing. It is the sun, the moon, the earth, and the ocean. It is also every person. *CCC, 279–280*

Q: What is the Blessed Trinity?

A: The Blessed Trinity is One God in Three Persons: God the Father, God the Son, and God the Holy Spirit. *CCC, 254, 261*

Q: What is faith?

A: Faith is a gift from God. It is only given to human beings. Faith helps us obey God and do what he wants us to do. *CCC, 153*

Q: What is an angel?

A: An angel is an invisible being that is a messenger of God. *CCC, 350*

CCC = Catechism of the Catholic Church

Q: **Who was Mary?**

A: God chose Mary to be the mother of Jesus. Mary is our mother, too. When we pray to Mary, we are asking her to talk to Jesus for us. *CCC, 509*

Q: **What does Christ mean?**

A: Christ is a name for Jesus that means "the chosen one of God." *CCC, 453, 454*

Q: **What is heaven?**

A: Heaven is life with God forever. *CCC, 665*

Q: **Who were the Apostles?**

A: The Apostles were twelve men Jesus chose to lead his followers. *CCC, 869*

Q: **What are priests and deacons?**

A: Priests are men who serve the Church by teaching and leading our prayers. Deacons are men who serve the Church by assisting priests and bishops. *CCC, 939*

Q: **What is prayer?**

A: Prayer is listening to and talking with God. *CCC, 2559*

Q: **What is liturgy?**

A: Liturgy is the work and prayer of the whole Church. *CCC, 1382, 1388*

Q: **What are sacraments?**

A: Sacraments are special signs Jesus gave to the Church to share God's life and love with us. *CCC, 1131*

Q: **What are sacramentals?**

A: Sacramentals are blessings, actions, and objects that help us live holy lives. *CCC, 1677*

Q: What is the Mass?

A: The Mass is the Church's most important celebration. *CCC, 1193*

Q: What is a parish?

A: A parish is a community within the Church that worships God together. *CCC, 804, 805, 810*

Q: What are saints?

A: Saints are people who led holy lives and now live happily forever with God. *CCC, 828*

Q: What are blessings and devotions?

A: A blessing is a prayer that asks God to make someone or something holy. A devotion is a form of personal or communal prayer. *CCC, 2590, 2591, 2645, 2721*

Q: What is Baptism?

A: Baptism is the first sacrament we receive, which gives us new life in Jesus. *CCC, 1213*

Q: What is grace?

A: Grace is God's life in us. *CCC, 1996–97, 2000*

Q: What is Confirmation?

A: Confirmation is the sacrament that strengthens us with the Gift of the Holy Spirit. *CCC, 1316*

Q: What is the Last Supper?

A: The Last Supper is the meal that Jesus shared with his followers on the night before he died. *CCC, 1323*

Q: What is the Eucharist?

A: The Eucharist is the sacrament of the Body and Blood of Jesus Christ. The Eucharist brings us more fully into the Church. *CCC, 1409, 1416*

Q: **What is sin?**

A: Sin is any thought, word, or action that we do on purpose even though we know that it is wrong.
CCC, 1849–50

Q: **What is Penance and Reconciliation?**

A: Penance and Reconciliation is the sacrament in which we receive and celebrate God's forgiveness.
CCC, 1440, 1422

Q: **What is Anointing of the Sick?**

A: Anointing of the Sick is the sacrament in which the priest prays for the Holy Spirit to bring God's comfort and peace to those who are sick.
CCC, 1518, 1527, 1528

Q: **What is Holy Orders?**

A: Holy Orders is the sacrament in which a baptized man becomes a deacon, a priest, or a bishop. These men share the message of Jesus, teach us about our faith, and help us to live as Jesus did. CCC, 1593

Q: **What is Matrimony?**

A: Matrimony is the sacrament through which a baptized man and a baptized woman become husband and wife. They promise to love and to be faithful to each other always. They love each other as Christ loves his Church. CCC, 1660–61

Q: **What is the Holy Family?**

A: The Holy Family is the family of Jesus, Mary, and Joseph. CCC, 1655

Q: **What are commandments?**

A: Commandments are laws that God gave us. They help us to know how God wants us to live.
CCC, 2081–82

Q: What is the Great Commandment?

A: The Great Commandment is Jesus' teaching to love God, ourselves, and others. Jesus showed us how to follow the Great Commandment by everything he said and did. **CCC, 1985**

Q: What are virtues?

A: Virtues are good habits that help us act as God wants us to. They help us make good choices. **CCC, 1833, 1840–42**

Q: What are the Ten Commandments?

A: The Ten Commandments are ten special laws God gave to his people. They are written in the Bible. We show our love for God, ourselves, and others by obeying the Ten Commandments. **CCC, 2056**

Q: What is the Lord's Day?

A: The Church calls Sunday the Lord's Day. One of the laws of the Church is that we should attend Mass on Sundays. This helps us make the Lord's Day holy, as the Ten Commandments tell us to do. **CCC, 1166–67**

Q: What is Original Sin?

A: Original Sin is the first sin. It was committed when the first man and woman, Adam and Eve, disobeyed God. **CCC, 1707**

Q: What is mercy?

A: Mercy is God's love and forgiveness. **CCC, 1987, 2018**

Q: What does invite mean?

A: Invite means to ask someone to do something. God invites all people to open their hearts and minds to him. God never stops calling or inviting each person to prayer. **CCC, 2591**

Q: **What is praise?**

A: Praise is prayer that shows respect for God and his greatness. *CCC, 2644*

Q: **When does God want us to pray?**

A: God wants us to pray always. He wants us to pray in good times and bad times, when we are happy and when we are sad. We should pray when things are busy and noisy, and when things are calm and quiet. *CCC, 2694, 2720, 2721, 2754, 2757*

Q: **What is the Lord's Prayer?**

A: The Lord's Prayer is the prayer that Jesus taught his followers. *CCC, 2774, 2776*

Index